Mama, Pray Me Home
Story of a Stolen Teenager

"Mama,
pray me home"

Lee Sturgeon

Belleville, Ontario, Canada

MAMA, PRAY ME HOME
Copyright © 2005, Lee Sturgeon

Library and Archives Canada Cataloguing in Publication

Sturgeon, Lee, 1956-
   Mama, pray me home / Lee Sturgeon.

ISBN 1-55306-926-9.--ISBN 1-55306-928-5 (LSI ed.)

   1. Sturgeon, Lee, 1956- 2. Camp meetings--United States. 3. Christian Biography. 4. Kidnapping victims--Biography. I. Title.

BV3785.S76A3 2005   269'.24'092   C2005-902918-8

Author photo courtesy of K. Sturgeon

For more information or
to order additional copies, please contact:

Lee Sturgeon
P.O. Box 970
Krum, TX 76249

Guardian Books is an imprint of *Essence Publishing,* a Christian Book Publisher dedicated to furthering the work of Christ through the written word.. For more information, contact:
   20 Hanna Court, Belleville, Ontario, Canada K8P 5J2
   Phone: 1-800-238-6376 • Fax: (613) 962-3055
   E-mail: publishing@essencegroup.com
   Internet: www.essencegroup.com

Printed in Canada
by

Guardian B O O K S

To my wife, Kathie: For all your love and devotion.

To my sons, Clint and Daniel, and their families:
You all are the greatest!

To my sisters, Barbara, Betty, and Lavona:
For never giving up on me.

To the endless list of family and friends who love me.

To the memory of my mom,
Mamie Maurine Sawyer Sturgeon
1916–1999

Introduction

This book is based on a true story. The names have been changed for the protection of all involved. It would serve no earthly good to use the actual names.

My hope is that by sharing this experience with people, young and old, who are vulnerable to influences outside of the realm of safety, I can help someone make some correct choices. If you face difficult decisions in your life today, I pray that you can find the strength to make choices with the understanding that God wants the best for your life. Your most important decision is to follow Him.

My sincere prayer is that someone who reads this story will take to heart the idea that when we pray—individually or corporately—for some person or situation, we should expect to see those prayers answered. God hears us. He cares. He has given us instructions to pray fervently when we have, or see, a need. My mother realized that, and that leads me to my reason for the title *"Mama, Pray Me Home."*

I want to take this opportunity to honor my mother for praying for her family. She prayed many prayers for all of us. The memories are as clear to me as if I had heard her pray today. I thank God for all of those times I heard her pray. And I thank God for listening.
God bless you.

Chapter One

I remember the Sunday morning service when the visitor came to church. I was sitting in my position behind the piano player, playing my bass guitar in the band. The choir finished the last song and took their seats. Our pastor stood to greet the congregation and the visitors. He read a name off a business card he had been handed before the service. He then asked the visitor to say a word to the congregation.

A short, somewhat stocky, middle-aged man with light brown hair stood and thanked the pastor. Then he addressed the congregation.

"Good morning," he said. "I am blessed to be here with all of you." He went on to tell us that he was a traveling preacher, a "tent evangelist," and his team had stopped in our town en route to somewhere else. I noticed that he seemed to have a smirk on his lips when he spoke.

He continued, "I appreciate your pastor's kindness. In the short amount of time I have known him and his wife, I can tell they are good people." He paused to wait for an "amen" from the congregation, which he got. "I feel a kindred spirit among us in this service. May God bless all of you."

I listened to him and watched him sit back down when he finished. The service continued, and I thought no more about it. I had more important things on my mind.

*

It was a hot July day in Abilene, Texas. The summer had been great so far, all things considered. Just out of the tenth grade, I spent most of the month of June mowing lawns around my neighborhood to earn some money for the summer. I spent most of July with two of my sisters in different parts of the state. My cousin Mark came to my sister's house in central Texas and picked me up on his motorcycle to take me to Dallas to attend his wedding.

I always had fun with Mark. Seven years older than me, he always had a motorcycle or a hot rod to pique my interest. He had also introduced me to some interesting girls. At the wedding I met Sue, a friend of his new wife. We hung around together some after the wedding and promised to stay in touch. Two days later, Mark took me back home.

I had now been home a couple of weeks. I had managed to mow a few more yards in the neighborhood to make some spending money.

I tried to keep a little money in my pocket for snacks and gas in case my best friend, Curtis, picked me up to run around town. I never knew when he would swing by. He worked at a bowling alley with his mom and had his own car.

Curtis and I had been buddies since we met in math class in the eighth grade. From that point on, we tried to take the same classes. He even signed up for choir although he was not a great singer. Some classes we could not take together, because he was smarter than I was and would take stuff like algebra and trigonometry. He was more sensible than I was, too. He talked me out of some bad ideas I had about leaving home. I was lucky to have a friend who cared. We saw a lot of bad stuff happening around us—fights, drug overdoses, suicide, and teen pregnancy, to name a few. We wanted none of that scene. We just wanted to live the best we could and have fun. And we did manage to have fun most of the time, especially since he had bought a car.

I dreamed of having my own car. But any car I could afford to buy would be a fixer-upper, and I had no money to fix up a fixer-upper. So buying one right now would not make sense. I would have to settle for running around with Curtis or one of my other friends and try to save enough to buy one later.

*

Life at home had been good when I was a kid. Although my family was poor, we never failed to have food on the table. We lived a simple life. Daddy and Mama taught us Christian values, and we all went to church together. I was the youngest of four kids, and I was the only boy. Daddy worked; the girls went to school; and I stayed home with Mama, who spent her days cooking and cleaning house. At some time during each busy day, she would kneel and pray. She would pray for God to bless her family, keep us safe, and guide us through every day. I loved to hear Mama pray. I had a feeling that when she prayed God listened. Until I turned six, I could imagine no other way to spend a day.

Soon after I started first grade, Daddy severely injured his back on his job and Mama had to get a job outside the house. Daddy was told he would not work again, and he fought terribly with doctors and lawyers to get some money for his injury. He began to get bitter about everything and everybody. He quit going to church.

Since he couldn't hold down a full-time job, he did what he could to bring some money in. He raised and sold rabbits. He gathered and sold scrap iron. He raised vegetables in the garden so we would not have to buy all our food. Every year his health deteriorated, and he depended on me to help him do a lot of the physical work. It took a lot of play time away from me, but I learned to cope. By the summer of my twelfth birthday, arthritis and other problems had taken its toll, and we discovered he had started drinking to ease the pain. That same summer we moved to Abilene, Texas.

We lived in an old rock house Daddy had purchased. He bought it for almost nothing. He and I totally rebuilt the inside and added two rooms and a hall onto the back of it. Working with him became harder than ever because of his drinking.

Although he did not intend to become an alcoholic, the alcohol meant to take him down. It made him mean and abusive, and he argued endlessly with Mama and me when he was drunk. He was not physically abusive, but he used bitter words that cut like a knife. I could not deal with the change in him, and before long I became rebellious about it. I learned to cut back with my own words and attitudes. We fought terribly, and when Mama was not making a living for us, she was trying to keep peace in the home. It was a hard life for her.

By the time I was sixteen, life at home was almost unbearable. That was why I had spent a few weeks for the last three summers with my two sisters who lived away from Abilene—so we could all have some peace.

When I was in Abilene, I tried to spend as much of my time as possible with Curtis or other friends or visiting my youngest sister across town. I had other friends— mostly girls—that I would walk across town to see.

I walked almost everywhere in Abilene, from the extreme southeast side where we lived to the extreme northwest side where my sister and some friends lived. It was normal for me to walk fifteen or so miles in a day, going from one friend's house to another and back home. I was also dating a girl who lived in another town, and sometimes I would ride the bus to see her for the weekend.

If I did have to be at home, I would try to stay in my room as much as possible. There I would practice piano, read, build model cars, or listen to music.

My room was one of the two rooms across the front of the house. The other was the living room. Both of them had doors that opened to the front porch. I liked having access to the outside, because I could come in late at night without waking anyone in the house.

Sometimes late at night I would go out that door and sit on the curb in front of the house, wishing I could just get away for good. But at the same time I was worried about how Mama would make it if I were gone for good. The few weeks I was gone each summer was enough to make her worry about me, as if her own situation was not enough to worry about. So I was concerned about her and she about me.

Between working and the stress at home, Mama was just too tired to go to church. So my youngest sister and I went to a church across town. When she married, I went to church by myself. I decided to return to a little church Mama and I went to when we first moved to Abilene. It was about a block away from my house, so it was easy for me to walk there, even carrying an instrument. I played piano on Wednesday nights and guitar on Sundays.

Soon after I returned, however, the congregation decided to buy a different building in another part of town. So I relied on Mama to take me to the new church. At times someone from the church would pick me up for services. The old building went up for sale but did not sell quickly. It still sat empty.

I loved to play my music in church. And I still desired to be around good church-going people so I could try to keep some form of decency in my life. We had a great youth group, and I was involved in several activities with them.

While I was not a good role model for anyone, by far, I could have been a lot worse. I was rebellious in my heart, but I never got into trouble with the law. I never took drugs or got drunk. I knew people everywhere around who had alcohol and drugs of all kinds, and others who could show me a "good time" in other ways. But I saw enough of the effects of alcohol at home to not want that kind of activity. And I did not want the consequences of living "the wild life." I picked my school friends carefully, and we did not dabble in such things.

The main reason I did not get into all of the wrong influences that were everywhere around me was the fact that Mama still prayed every day for her family. Many nights I came home late, and when I opened my door, I could hear her in the little room in the center of the house—praying for me. It comforted me to know Mama mentioned my name in prayer.

God was merciful to us through all those dark days.

Chapter Two

On the Tuesday after the Sunday the visiting evangelist came to church, I walked from my house to a small store a couple of blocks over to get a snack. I passed by the little church building that had been the gathering place for our congregation for many years before we bought the big church in another part of town.

As I passed by, I saw a truck and trailer rig and an old bus in the side parking lot. Two cars sat out front. The big trailer was painted light blue with a sign in white letters that read "Soul-Saving Crusade—Healing—Miracles." It went on to give the name of the evangelist. The bus was the same color as the trailer.

I went on to the store. When I came back by, two guys were working under the hood of one of the cars, a Cadillac. I walked up behind the guys and, referring to the sign on the trailer, asked, "Is one of you guys Sam Eastly?"

One of them said, "Yeah. What about it?" He turned to me, and I recognized him as the man who had visited our church. I was so surprised at his abrupt answer that I almost turned and left then, but I pressed on with the course of the conversation instead.

Standing there in my bell-bottoms and sandals, I told him who I was and that I was at the church on Sunday when he spoke. He introduced me to the other guy, Gene. After a few minutes of talking about his ministry, we got around to the fact that I was a musician. He said he was looking for an organist to travel with them. I said that I was much better on the piano. He wanted to hear me play, so the three of us went in the church, through the back door, into the Sunday school rooms. As we went through, I was introduced to their families. Gene had four kids and a wife, Donna. Sam had one three-year-old son, and his wife, Julie, had twins on the way, he said.

I auditioned on the piano and sang, and he offered me the job.

"I could use you, if you are willing to travel. I'll give you seventy-five dollars per week if you will go to Arkansas with us for six weeks." He looked serious.

"Seventy-five dollars per week for six weeks?" I gasped. "Wow! That's almost five hundred bucks!" I struggled to slow my thoughts down. "I don't know if my parents will let me go, but it sounds good to me."

"Well, are your parents at home?" he asked.

"Daddy is. Mama will be there at 5:30. She works," I said.

"I could go talk to them, tell them the plan, and see if they will let you go. Surely they won't hold back a talented kid like you. Of course, they will have to sign a paper saying you can go, since you are a minor. I'll write one up."

"Well, okay," I said. Then I told him where I lived.

"Okay then. I'll be over about 6:00."

As I walked home, I got more excited every step. I said a selfish prayer that my parents would say I could go. Although I had only been home a short time, I was ready to leave again. Mama wouldn't like the thought of me going out of state with total strangers. But, strangers or not, making seventy-five dollars a week playing music sounded great to me. And I had never been to Arkansas. I was ready to go.

At the supper table, I knew I had to tell them about Sam. I dreaded it, but I could not let my dread deter me from accomplishing my mission—to get out of town and make some money.

"There's a tent evangelist staying at our old church."

Mama seemed interested. "Really? I wonder what he's doing there. Is his tent set up?"

"No. I stopped and talked to him and some other guy today. They were working on a car. They have a truck and trailer, a bus, and two cars. One of the cars is a Cadillac. It's cool!"

I hoped to get Daddy's attention by mentioning the impressive make of car. To this point, he ate silently. My plan failed. He just was not interested in what I had to say.

"He wants to hire me as an organist for six weeks. He'll pay me seventy-five dollars per week." I looked at both of them. "I—I want to go."

Mama dropped her fork and looked at me. Then she looked at Daddy, who looked up from his food and stared at me.

"What do you mean? Where is he going?" she asked.

"To Arkansas. I would be back in time for school. And I could save my money and use some for school stuff." That was *not* what I wanted to say, but I thought it might help win my case.

I continued. "He—the preacher—is coming over tonight to talk to y'all about it." I looked back-and-forth between them, hopeful that they would—by some miracle—agree that it was a grand idea.

Daddy finally spoke. "I need you around here for the rest of the summer."

My defenses were alerted. "What for?" I asked. "It's not like you have a lot to do. I haven't done much since I got back from Mark's. What is it going to hurt?"

Now it was Mama's turn. "Son, we can't let you go to Arkansas with somebody you just met. What do you know about him? What if you get into trouble?"

"I'm not going to get into trouble. I'm just going to play music. And I'm going to make some money. He seems like a nice guy. You'll meet him in a little while. Just wait until you talk to him to make up your mind. Okay?"

"Well, I doubt that it will help. But—we'll see."

And that was the end of it until Sam came.

He arrived when he said he would. My parents listened intently as he told them he had some revival meetings scheduled in Arkansas for a total of six weeks, and if I could go help him, he would have me home in time for school. After much talking between the four of us, they said I could go. They signed a handwritten note saying so, and plans were set in motion.

I was excited. It seemed to me that maybe this was

the break I had needed to get some extra money. After all, I *did* pray about it, and my parents *did* say yes.

*

The plan was for Gene to take the truck and trailer to Arkansas and ride a bus back to Abilene. His family would continue to stay in the duplex they had rented across the alley behind the church, waiting for him to return to prepare the bus for the trip, load up the supplies, his family, and now me. We were to head out the first part of August.

Sam asked me if I would stay a couple of nights in the back room of the church to make sure nothing was bothered while Gene was gone. I told him I would get Curtis to stay with me, not admitting that I was a little spooked to stay by myself in the back of a church.

On Saturday, July 29, Sam loaded up his family in the Caddy, Gene climbed in the truck, and they headed out.

During the days that followed, I went about my business but kept a watch on the church and Gene's family. Three nights of that week Curtis and I stayed there. We had a great time. Curtis brought a portable record player, and we both brought our favorite records and some snacks. It was kind of like camping out. Then in the mornings we would go home.

I went to my lawn-mowing customers and told them I would be leaving. One elderly couple listened with interest as I told them of my plans. They looked at one another when I told them who I was going with. They said they had met Sam. They told me to have fun and come back safe.

After Gene came back early Tuesday morning, I spent most of my time getting to know him and his family, helping them make preparations, and packing the bus. I loved buses. I had ridden on several, but not one like this. It was a 1954 GMC, Gene informed me. Most of the seats had been removed, soon to be replaced with the furniture and appliances we would build or buy in Arkansas.

I found him to be a mild-mannered guy. We made friends easily, and I enjoyed helping him with the preparations. He was an American Indian in his forties, a tad shorter than my six-foot height, and dark creases on his face showed years of hard living. He smoked cigarettes. Although I had smoked some for the past couple of years, I had been raised to believe it was wrong to do. I decided to keep my thoughts to myself. It was his business, not mine.

On the other hand, Donna made it clear every chance she could that she did not like his smoking. She was a nice lady. She was busy with the kids most of the time, and when she brought us sandwiches and drinks outside, she was cheerful. She also had some signs of rough living on her face. She was built small and was maybe an inch shorter than Gene. Her shoulders stooped a little, making her look tired, and she appeared some older than Gene. But when the kids were around, I could tell she enjoyed being a mom. She would do her best to make each one feel special. To me, all of the kids seemed a little rowdy. Three were boys— John, Robert, and David, ages two, four, and eight, respectively. Their daughter, Sarah, was six.

Chapter Three

On Wednesday morning of that week, Dad got drunk and told me I couldn't go. We had an argument about it, which ended with me locking myself up in my room. He changed his mind after he sobered up.

On Thursday, I was inside the church with Gene when a pickup pulled up to the curb. A guy got out and came to the door. Gene opened the door, and to my surprise, there stood my ninth-grade English teacher, Mr. Dean, holding a box of canned food. He looked at me like I was the last one he expected to see. He asked how I was doing and handed Gene the canned food. Then he was gone. When I had asked Gene what the food was for, he said we were taking up donations for underprivileged kids.

On Friday, I went to the church to help Gene. As I approached, he stepped out of the bus slowly and faced me.

He said, "Your dad visited me last night and said you cannot go with us." He watched my face for a response.

I was furious. I mumbled, "I'll be back." Then I went home and argued with my dad.

"Why?" I asked.

"It don't matter why."

"You already said I could go." My voice was rising. "You had no right to change your mind."

"I have every right."

"You are just afraid I'll have fun, and you want me to be here helping you!" They were the only rational accusations I could think of that might make him change his mind.

He wouldn't listen to me, so I got on my bike and rode thirty miles to my girlfriend's house. I told her parents about the trouble, and they listened. I thought they were on my side.

But the following morning, I heard a knock on their front door. Mom and Dad stood there. I was told to go with them. It was clear I was in this alone. On the way home, I convinced Mom and Dad that they ought to let me go.

After we got home, I went to tell Gene. He listened quietly with his head down. "I don't want to cause trouble," he said.

"You're not causing trouble. It's just him. I promise you, I will go. I'll handle Daddy. Don't worry about it."

"Well, whether you go or not, I have to pull out tonight," he said frankly.

"I'll be here," I responded.

I got excited all over again! I went home and packed a few clothes in a cardboard box, along with some eight-track tapes and other things I thought I would need.

That evening, I looked around my room one last time and convinced myself everything would be in order when I got back. The pale-green walls were lined with pictures of race cars I had cut out of hot rod magazines, along with some pictures of my cousin's Super Bee at the drag strip. I had helped him build it and was very proud to be a part of the experience. The old dark-brown piano against the wall had been inherited from my grandma. It had served three purposes: it had provided a place for me to develop my musical talent; it had provided some inner peace for me when I played it; and it had made a great shelf for the many model cars I had built over the last few years. They sat there now side by side, the molded plastic headlights staring at me as if they knew I was leaving.

I walked into the kitchen, said good-bye to my unemotional dad, hugged my tearful mama, and headed to the church.

We pulled out at 10:00 p.m. I rode in the Plymouth Fury with his wife and kids, and he drove the bus. I decided it was going to be a rough trip for me if I had to spend all my time with the kids. Not that I didn't like kids. I enjoyed being around my nephews and cousins. But these were different to me. They were basically strangers. They were rowdy in the car. Besides, I wanted to ride in the bus some.

As we made the loop around Abilene, I realized that we were headed west. I knew that Arkansas was east of Texas.

I asked Donna, "Why are we going west, when Arkansas is east?"

Her voice had a defensive tone as she answered, "Well, maybe Gene knows a better way. I'm just following him."

I looked at her a moment, but she never looked my way, and I knew she was saying nothing else. I was not entirely sure what was going on, but I said no more about it. I decided I would ask Gene about it.

We stopped at a truck stop about forty miles west of Abilene. As we came to a stop at a gas pump, I headed straight for the bus.

"Gene, I thought we were going to Arkansas. We are going west."

"Well, Lee," he spoke softly as he fought with the hose and started the gas pumping into the big tank on the bus, "I guess we need to talk a little about it. Let's wait until we are inside."

I shuffled around the bus, anxious to hear what he had to say.

He waited until we were seated in the booth in the café before he spoke. He lit up a cigarette and reluctantly told me, "We are headed to Wyoming, not Arkansas. Sam didn't want me to tell you."

"Wyoming?" I was shocked. "But my parents think I'm going to Arkansas. That's what they were told."

"You can call them when we get there. I'm sure they won't mind."

I was not that sure about it. I quietly wrestled with the situation for a while. Mama was a worrier. I was sure she was worried about me at that moment. If she knew the plans were all a lie, she would not sleep at all. They thought we were going in a totally opposite direction. The paper they had signed had plainly said "Arkansas."

*

Back in the car, we pulled out on the interstate. I watched the lights of distant buildings and communities pass as I pondered my situation.

Although Mama was a natural-born worrier, and she was handed a lot of things to worry about in this life, she was still a praying lady. She had faith in God. Although I did not exactly live up to all of the values I knew were right, and although my home had not felt much like a Christian home lately, I still had respect for God—and for Mama. I had seen times when that faith was all that kept her nerves together during trouble in the family. I remembered the times I would walk in the front door and hear Mama praying for me. I knew God understood and honored her faith.

I had heard somewhere that God keeps prayers and tears bottled up, and He can open up the bottle and take out what is needed at any given time. I knew He surely had many bottled-up tears and prayers from her.

As I contemplated all of this in my mind, I settled down to enjoy seeing the lights of places I had never seen. The thought of leaving behind the trouble at home made me feel better. I was tired of the bad words between Daddy and myself. After all, I could not get out of the car and walk back to the house now.

Six weeks in Arkansas or Wyoming—what is the difference? I thought to myself.

Chapter Four

It seemed like we drove forever that first night. I fell asleep somewhere in west Texas and woke up as we pulled over at a roadside park somewhere in New Mexico not long before daylight. Gene made a pot of coffee and opened a gallon can of beef stew that had been donated in Abilene.

As we ate the stew, I remembered the day at the old church when Mr. Dean brought the food donation. I thought of the puzzled look he gave me, and the thought of it bothered me.

"You want some coffee to go with that?" Donna's voice brought me back to the present.

I didn't even drink coffee, but this seemed like a great time to start. "Sure, I'll try some," I answered.

It was a very cool night there in the mountains, and the hot stew and coffee warmed me up inside. I felt like a true adventurer. I liked the coolness and the mountains. It reminded me of times when I was very young. We had taken several trips to Arizona to see my grandpa, and I had loved mountains ever since. This night in New Mexico, it was so peaceful and quiet. It seemed so far from the trouble I had seen at home.

After we ate, Donna made the kids get on the bus and go back to sleep. Sitting there around the fire, I told Gene about how the trouble between Daddy and me got started. It seemed easy to talk about it in this remote place under the stars.

In turn, he told me a little about himself.

"I've done about everything there is to do, I guess. I was raised on a farm. When I got grown, I left to live on my own. Then I married my first wife. I drove trucks for a living for several years. I traveled everywhere around this country. It was a hard life. I lost my first wife because I was gone so much. I played in some bands, worked odd jobs, and tried different things in different places, but always wound up back home working on my dad's farm in Oklahoma. That is where I met Donna. She was a waitress at a café I went to."

"So how did you meet Sam?"

"I have traveled with Sam before. It has been several years. We didn't get along, so I left him."

"So why did you come back with him?" I asked.

Gene thought quietly for a moment. "Well, I thought I would give him another try. We had some good times in spite of the trouble, and he needs me to make this run for him. He's had time to change, and I think maybe he has."

We slept there at the roadside park. I slept in the car. Gene and Donna slept in the bus with the kids.

The next day on the road, the bus started overheating. Steam began to pour from the radiator cap atop the bus. Donna flashed the Fury's lights, and Gene started slowing down. I heard him rev up the engine a few times. I could hear the big engine spit and cough. Then we saw the bus pulling over to the side of the road.

Gene knew a lot about working on vehicles, and he said the old bus needed some major work. But we had to get to Wyoming.

"I just hope the thing makes it to Laramie before it blows," he said thoughtfully as he examined the opened engine area. "Then maybe we'll have time and money to fix it right. For now, I'll have to get some jugs to keep water in the radiator." He closed the engine door, gathered up the kids from playing, and told Donna to get them into the car.

Then he addressed me, saying, "Lee, stay here on the bus while we go get something put water in. If anyone stops, tell them we're broke down, but don't let them know you're alone if you don't have to. We'll be back soon."

I watched them drive away, then turned and sat on the top step in the open bus doorway. *Sure, I'll stay here alone,* I thought. *I could use some peace and quiet!*

They were back inside of an hour. He drove the Fury up to the back of the bus as close as he could. Everybody piled out of the car, and he called me to help him retrieve the three five-gallon cans he had purchased to keep water in. They were filled.

"Climb up on the hood of the car, Lee," he said, "and pour this water in the radiator. Pour it slowly so you won't spill it. I think we'll be doing this pretty often."

I carefully poured the water from one can, then the next, until the radiator was full. He started the engine and allowed time for the water to flow through the engine. The water level dropped as the engine warmed up. I poured more in, until I knew it would hold no more.

"Okay, let's go. We'll stop and fill the jugs again. I'll watch the temperature gauge. If I pull over, Donna, you pull up to the bus like I did, and let Lee pour the water in. We'll leave the radiator cap loose. Maybe that will help."

So that started a ritual that would last until we got to Laramie. He watched the gauges on the dash of the bus, and every now and again he would have to pull over. Donna would pull the Fury right behind the bus. I would get on the hood of the car with the water can and fill the radiator. Then, as Gene drove on, we would stop to get more water, then catch up with him.

Although I did not have a license to drive, sometimes Gene allowed me to drive to relieve Donna. The Fury was a nice car, a '67 model. I knew some about cars.

My dad began to teach me to drive when I was ten years old. Back when we got along good. Back before he started drinking. Also, during the last two summers when I stayed with one sister, she let me drive around their small town. I gained some good experience there. Then my youngest sister had let me drive her car when she was still at home, because I'd made a deal to keep it clean if she would let me. And my cousin Mark had let me drive several of his cars, including the Super Bee he raced.

But now I was driving a car full of someone else's kids, and that made me nervous. I kept my eyes open for police.

We didn't make it far in New Mexico that day. We were still traveling after dark, and I was still driving the Fury. A cop came up behind me with his lights flashing. I eased over, heart pounding. *What did I do?* I thought. *How could he know I have no license? What will they do to me? I am definitely not on the good side of the law driving without a license!*

The lights went flashing by me and pulled back into the lane in front of me behind the bus. Gene pulled over. I stopped back away from the bus, hoping they wouldn't come to the car. In a few minutes, I saw Gene and the policeman walking to the back of the bus. They stopped and looked at the tag on the back of the bus. I breathed easier when the cop got back in his car and pulled out. Gene waved and returned to the driver's seat of the bus. He told us at the next rest stop that the cop was checking the fifteen-day Texas tag, making sure that we were legal and that we were just passing through.

We continued to gas up at truck stops, because they were roomy enough for the bus and because Gene was used to truck stops. I enjoyed being around the big trucks, and the smell of diesel intrigued me.

We slept in the car and bus every night. The kids would get tired of being cooped up, and I got tired of being cooped up with them. But I was beginning to like them. John and Robert were funny little guys, always wanting attention. Sarah enjoyed laughing and would giggle at anything remotely humorous. David was a protective big brother but a little sulky when he was not getting the respect he thought he deserved.

Chapter Five

We spent the third night at a rest stop outside of Trinidad, Colorado. I met Gene outside the bus just after daylight. We heard a motorcycle drive up and turned to see it as the rider pulled right up to a covered picnic table about fifty yards from us. He was wearing a Hell's Angels vest.

We kept watching as he got off the bike and lay across the table. Then we went into the bus where Donna had been preparing breakfast.

When we stepped back off the bus, the rider was back on his bike, smoking a cigarette. His back was to us. Gene motioned for me to follow him. He said, "Let's go talk to him a minute."

I said, "Man, you're crazy! He's a Hell's Angel. He'll kill us!"

"Naw, he don't look dangerous," he said as he kept walking. I followed. We made a wide swing so the rider could see us before we got to him. He threw us a glance as we walked up, and Gene spoke in a low, easy tone.

"Morning," Gene said.

"Hey," he answered, taking another drag on the cigarette.

"Nice bike. Where you headed?" Gene asked as he lit up a cigarette of his own.

The guy looked to be in his early twenties and, in spite of his attire, looked like a regular, peaceable guy. I just stood back looking at him and the bike, ready to run if I had a reason to.

"Going to L.A."

Not a man for words, I thought.

"Long trip. It's been a while since I was out there. Used to drive a truck across the states. I was out there several times."

The guy didn't act too interested. "Yeah, well, I'd better be goin'." He stood on the kick-starter and dropped as the huge Harley roared to life. He nodded as he pushed it back a few feet and pulled onto the asphalt. I looked at Gene, who still looked after the bike, now well across the park and hitting the service road. I thought I saw a hint of envy in his eyes for a quick moment.

We took the interstate north through Colorado, still pampering the overheating bus. As I drove behind the bus, I enjoyed taking glances at the mountains to the left of us as we drove north to Wyoming.

*

We made it to Laramie, Wyoming, before daylight Friday, some five days after leaving Abilene. We stopped beside the road at the south edge of town. After daylight, Gene took the Fury into town and called Sam, who came to meet us.

As he stepped out of the Caddy, Sam seemed relieved to see us. He looked at me and said, "Well, I see you decided to come with us."

"Yeah, it is good to be here," I said cautiously. I thought to myself that he must have figured I would have changed my mind when I found out we were not going to Arkansas. I remembered Daddy changing his mind twice and wondered if it had been a sign I should not have come after all. I looked around at the mountains around us and quickly shook the thought out of my mind.

He led us to the motel where they were staying. We went to their room and spent the day with him and his family. We ate sandwiches for lunch.

"I met a preacher who will help us during our time here," Sam said to Gene over lunch. "He pastors a small congregation on the north side. We'll park everything in the space behind the church until we get a place to set up the tent."

Gene seemed pleased with the arrangement. "Are we going to work on the bus there? We need to get that started with Sister Julie about to deliver."

"Yeah. We will stay at the motel until we can move into the bus. I've made arrangements for you, Donna, and the kids in the back rooms of the church. Meanwhile, we'll buy the stuff to work on the bus." Sam looked my direction. "You don't mind sleeping in the trailer for a few days, do you, Lee? We've got the front of it fixed up real nice like an office with a couch, desk, and carpet."

"Naw, I don't mind." *Anything is better than a car for now,* I thought to myself.

He got Gene and his family a room for that night. They put me in the big blue trailer behind the truck, left me a flashlight, and latched the door from the outside. I could not get out. I didn't care until the next morning, when I woke up needing the restroom. I beat on the trailer walls for a long time. No one came. I hollered. I could hear nothing outside. I was getting mad, scared and miserable. I was locked up like an animal. Had they left me and gone somewhere else? I didn't know.

Gene finally came and let me out. He said they just didn't hear me. I was still mad for a while, but I got over it. Gene's calm disposition made me feel better when he was around. But I already had some reservations about Sam.

Saturday we moved all the equipment to the church he had talked about. The pastor and his family were there when we pulled up in the truck. He was a big, friendly-looking black man named Ivan. His wife, Grace, was white. They both appeared to be in their thirties. They had three children, all younger than me. Sam introduced everyone, and we went in to check out the apartment in the back where Gene and his family would be staying.

Stepping back outside, Brother Ivan said to me, "Well, you're a lot younger than these other men, Lee. Are you kin to one of them?"

"No sir. I was hired as a musician. I'm just with them for a few weeks. I'm sixteen and live in Texas." Realizing he probably didn't want to know everything about me, I fell silent as Sam came out discussing plans with Gene.

We attended their Sunday services. It was a small church, with about twenty folks in attendance, both blacks and whites. They invited me to sing. Then we ate with them, and I enjoyed visiting with the kids.

Chapter Six

The next two weeks were very busy. We spent a lot of time converting the bus into a camper. We built a dining booth on the left side, about the center of the seating area. We built cabinets and installed a sink. We ran the plumbing under the bus and installed a waste tank. Gene told me we would do more when we were between services.

During that time, Sam was looking for a place to set up the tent. He found a place across from a big park. We got the permit to set up, so we moved the bus, truck, and trailer to the site. Sam and his family moved into a nicer motel. Gene and his family moved into the bus.

Suddenly I found out that my duties were to involve more than playing music and working on the bus.

Sam told Gene and I, "I normally hire winos off the street to set up the tent. But we're low on money, so we're going to do it."

The three of us drove the stakes on a Sunday morning. Then we laid the tent out, sat the center posts, pulled and tugged on the ropes until the tent stood erect, and tied it off. That took the biggest part of the day.

On Monday, Gene moved the big trailer just outside one end of the tent, and we took the big plywood stage sections out of the trailer and put it all together at that end of the tent. Brother Ivan had a pickup and trailer we could use to haul some sawdust in. We went to a sawmill close by and got a couple of loads to spread on the floor under the tent.

I spotted two teenage girls watching what was going on from the outside of the tent. During a break, I introduced myself.

"Hi. My name is Lee."

"Hi. I'm Karen. This is Linda."

"Hi, Linda."

"Hi," she said shyly.

"Well, do y'all live around here?" I wasn't the best at meeting new girls—never had been good at it.

"Yeah." Karen gestured behind her. "I live over there around the corner."

Linda added, pointing beyond the park, "Yeah, and I live two blocks that way."

I nodded. "Well, it's good to meet you both. I'm from Texas."

"Texas?" Karen gasped. "I've never been there!"

Gene walked up, and I introduced everyone. He turned to me. "I'm sorry to interrupt, but it's time to eat."

"Well, okay." Turning to Karen, whom I immediately liked, I said, "I've got to go eat."

"Okay. We had better go."

"Okay, cool! Come back sometime. We'll be having service here for a couple of weeks, I think."

"Okay, see you later." They both waved as they walked toward Karen's house.

I walked with Gene to the bus to eat.

*

Tuesday we unloaded the organ, drums, guitars, public-address system, pulpit, and altars. Lastly, we set up the folding chairs and literature tables.

Once the setting up was done, Sam sent Gene and I to a Salvation Army store on the corner down the street to get some dress clothes for me. All I had brought from home were casual shirts and bell-bottom pants. Gene helped me pick out some dress slacks and a few sport coats.

The following day, a photographer came and took our pictures. Sam said he would get some posters made up with the pictures on them.

Then Sam told me my next job. "Lee, I need you to get the cot out of the trailer and sleep in the tent to watch the equipment. You can sleep on the stage. I don't expect trouble, but just in case anyone gets curious enough to pay us a late night visit, someone needs to be out here."

By this time, I felt I knew Gene well enough to confide in him a little, so I talked to him about it. "I don't know if I'm going to like staying here in the tent at night."

"I will stay out here with you some, but you will be okay," Gene reassured me.

I spent some time during the next couple of days practicing on the organ, since I had not played one that much. It was a small, simple Baldwin, and I got comfortable on it quickly. We had a small PA system with three microphones. Gene was a guitarist, and Sam played the drums, so we practiced some together. Sam sang some songs that he wanted Gene and I to learn for the services, and they learned some of mine.

Sam told me he wanted me to play the organ softly behind his preaching. "But when you hear me raise my voice," he said, "increase the volume. When I lower my voice, you decrease the volume again. See? It's a way to get the audience excited."

I nodded that I understood.

The morning the pictures were delivered, Sam and I had an argument over money. I wasn't getting paid the seventy-five dollars per week I had been promised. In fact, I hadn't been paid anything.

"Sam," I said to him under the tent, "when am I going to get paid?"

He looked at me with sharp, beady eyes. "You'll get paid when we start making money in the offerings."

"Well, you said I'd get seventy-five dollars per week, and I'm not getting it. So, I will expect what you owe me from the start of this trip."

"What?" I thought he was going to jump out of his skin, he yelled so loud. "You don't get paid for the time we were not in services. I told you I'd pay you to play the organ, remember? And I *am* feeding you, by the way!"

"That's not what you said before we left Abilene. You said I'd be gone for six weeks, and I'd get seventy-five dollars a week. That's why I came."

"Well, you misunderstood, kid." He stared hard at me. "You don't get paid when I don't get paid." He stomped to the bus and disappeared inside.

"Well, you lied, Mister!" I fired back as I walked away. I went to the truck, turned on the stereo, and sulked. I had been there a while when I saw him through the mirror.

He walked up to the door. "Come with me," he said in a stern voice.

I climbed down the steps and followed him at a distance.

He motioned for me to get in the back seat of the Cadillac. Julie was in the front passenger seat.

"Get in," he said.

"Where are we going?" I asked, still seething.

"We're going downtown to get posters made."

We rode in silence for a couple of blocks, then he started in again. "I am feeding you three meals a day. We are not making any money yet, so I don't have any money to pay you."

"You promised seventy-five dollars per week for six weeks. That was the deal we made," I snapped, not hiding my feelings.

He snapped back, "Seventy-five dollars per week for playing the organ. Have you been playing the organ? Huh?"

"No. But I have been working. I helped set up the tent. I've done your odd jobs."

We parked at the print shop. I started to get out.

"Stay in the car. I'll do this myself." He threw a glance at his wife as he got out and slammed the door.

Julie was a Southern lady with an Alabama accent. She had dark brown hair that curled at the ends below her shoulders. She was pretty. She was taller than he

43

was, I had noticed. And she was silly enough to stand up for him. She looked at me and smiled.

"Lee," she said in a concerned voice, "you know he's trying to do the best he can. He can't afford to pay you when we're not making money. You should not get mad at him. He's really a nice guy. He don't want to fight with you."

I felt hot tears running down my face. "I don't want to fight, either. I've had all I want of that at home with my old man. That's why I wanted to go with y'all, besides making some money. But he owes me."

"Well, he says you misunderstood him about that. He can't pay you between services."

She spoke so softly that she calmed me down. But I was not convinced of what she was saying. She was sure crazy about this man. That was for sure. I wondered what he had promised her. She was as dumb as a rock if she really thought I believed he was such a great guy.

We sat in silence until Sam came back out of the print shop and eased into the car. He looked at me through the mirror, then looked at Julie. She smiled at him and said, "It's all worked out now."

I looked out of the window and said nothing all the way back to the tent. I was in a hard place. I knew I was fighting a losing battle, and I did not like losing. I had to figure out how to make the best of it.

We continued to eat a lot of those donated cans of food, along with a few groceries bought at a local store. Turns out, we seemed to be the "underprivileged."

Chapter Seven

We started services on Thursday, August 31. Every day we were to have an afternoon service at one o'clock and an evening service at seven o'clock. Several folks came, including some preachers from various churches in town. They all seemed to enjoy the services, which included singing, testimonies, receiving an offering, preaching, and praying for the sick and unsaved.

During the preaching, Sam had to motion to me several times the first night when he wanted me to increase the organ volume. He would hold his right arm down at his side and wiggle his fingers until he heard the music swell.

The second night, I saw Karen sitting on the second row of chairs. I had been glancing at her when I caught a glimpse of Sam turning toward me and scowling as he stood by the altar. I apparently missed a signal. I acted like I was not caught by surprise at all and pressed the pedal. His faced relaxed, and he turned back to the people and continued.

Karen and I began to spend some time together, although our time was limited because school had started. She became my only friend my age in Laramie. She would stay around after service and help us cover up the instruments. Then we would talk about our lives and our schools as I walked her home. We'd sit on her back porch until her mom called her in. Then I'd walk back to the tent and sleep on the cot.

*

Work on the bus continued. We installed a small refrigerator and stove. Then we built a bed in the back and glued carpet squares on the floor. It was not a professional job, but it didn't look bad. We also did some engine work, trying to take care of the overheating problem. Gene said the head gasket must be broken, so we took the motor apart and found a busted head. Gene found one at a wrecking yard. We rebuilt it and put the whole thing back together.

The weather had become volatile. It rained almost every other day. When it rained, the wind would blow hard. The ground was getting soggy. The temperature ranged from the 40s to the 70s. Sometimes it would be sunny in the morning and rain all afternoon. Gene and I had to keep the tent ropes tight. So we would get out in the rain and wind, untying and retying ropes and driving stakes deeper into the ground. It was a hard, wet job, and I wished it would just dry up for a while. I had done hard work before but never work as muddy or demanding as trying all hours of the day and night to keep the tent up.

I was getting at least a little homesick. Except for days we worked on the bus or hammering tent stakes, I spent some of my time sitting in the cab of the truck listening to eight-track tapes. There I could be alone and think. I wondered how things were going at home. I was sure in a different situation here. At least at home I got a steady allowance—not much, but steady. Here, Sam had started giving me five dollars here and there, and I'd rush to the store and get a snack.

One day, sitting there in the truck, I wrote my parents a letter. I mentioned it to Sam and told him I wanted to mail it. He told me to give all my letters to him, and he would bundle them up with his and send them to Maryland. The secretary in his office there would mail them to Texas. I couldn't understand why. I wanted to call them, to let Mama know where I was. He told me I couldn't. He said I needed to wait until we were in an area where we were going to stay for a while.

The services seemed to be going okay. In spite of my suspicions of Sam, I watched as several people's spiritual and physical needs seemed to get met in the services. I had been in church all my life, and I knew when God showed up in the services. I could not understand why He would show up if Sam were such a bad guy. So I tried to keep a positive feeling about Sam's ministry. It was not easy.

One lady in particular who had begun coming to the services came up for prayer one night and said her back was giving her a lot of trouble. She walked with a limp because of it. Sam and some others gathered around her and prayed. Sam said that she had one leg shorter than the other leg and that she would receive her healing that night. They prayed again, and she seemed to be better. Her name was Ellen Riley. She had an eleven-year-old daughter named Pam who came with her. They came back almost every night, and Ellen spent a lot of extra time with the team between services. Sam announced one day that Ellen would be doing some secretary-type work for us. He and Julie showed her what to do.

I remembered the way Sam treated Brother Ivan when we first came to Laramie. It seemed to me like he took advantage of Ivan's kindness. I thought about the money I was supposed to have made so far and how I had been cheated—Gene and his family, too. I saw Ellen becoming the next victim. I was beginning to see that was how he treated everyone around him.

The people who would come to the services were not giving enough money to support us, and in spite of all his efforts and contacts he had made in town, even a sixteen year old could see Sam getting impatient and abrupt. His sermons became more about "giving and supporting the ministry" than "salvation and healing." I think people got tired of hearing it, because the crowds dropped off.

Julie delivered their twins, and Sam was going crazy trying to handle everything. He was becoming increasingly moody, and I stayed away from him when I could.

Gene sold the Fury to a man who had been attending the services. I knew he hated to see it go, but he had to feed his family.

We ran the services eleven days and closed out on a Sunday night in the middle of a huge rainstorm. We were afraid the tent was going to blow down, and we enlisted the help of everyone who could to help us get the instruments into the trailer. Karen and Linda were there working frantically with us to get the chairs, instruments, and tables into the trailer. I slept in the Caddy that night.

We dismantled and loaded the stage on Monday. We took the soggy tent down on Tuesday and packed it away, knowing that we would have to unfold it at the earliest opportunity to let it dry out. From the looks of the sky, that was not going to happen soon.

Karen came to see me one last time before we pulled out. I hated to lose this friend who had spent so much time with me. I had talked to her more than I had to any female friend back home.

"Well, I guess this is it. We have got to head out for somewhere down the road. Can I take a picture?" I held up my Kodak instant camera.

"Okay," she said. She stood up against the trailer as I snapped the picture.

"I'll miss you. I need your address," I said as I fumbled with a pen and paper. "I'll write you when I can," I said. "Will you write me back?"

She nodded. "Yes, I'll write you."

We hugged and exchanged a friendly kiss. Then I climbed into the truck. She waved as we pulled onto the road. I knew I would miss being with her, but there was nothing I could do except keep my promise to write.

We parked everything at a campground west of town and stayed there for a week. During that time, we managed to dry out the tent

We had been in the Laramie area six weeks when we headed out on another stormy day. Sam said we were going further west, to Idaho.

Chapter Eight

It was mid September. I was supposed to have been home for school a week before. Instead, we were headed to another state, and I had talked to no one at home. I could not imagine what my parents were going through. I wasn't too worried about Dad. He wouldn't miss me anyway, I thought. But I knew Mama needed to know. The letter I had sent was the only way they had heard from me, and in that letter I had told them I was okay. And I had told them I was in Wyoming. But at the time I had written it, I did not know I would not be home at the appointed time.

I started to protest about not heading for Texas, but thought better of it. I decided to just go along for the ride. I would call home and explain when I got a chance.

I did enjoy being on the road. That part of the country is so different from anything I had seen in Texas. The scenery was beautiful. I was amazed at the size of the mountains we were driving through. Although I was a little homesick, and I knew I should be easing through my junior year back at Abilene High, I did not miss fighting with Dad. Although Sam and I were getting on each other's nerves about like Dad and I did and I was not comfortable about the way I was being treated by him, at least I did not have to deal with alcoholism.

Donna was to drive the Caddy. Her kids were with her. Gene and I were in the truck. Sam and his family were on the bus. Before we pulled out of the campground, I relayed a message to Sam from Gene.

"Gene said to watch those gauges close, especially the temperature gauge. He's not sure how it is going to do on the open road."

"All right, all right!" He was ready to leave and clearly agitated at the time it was taking to get on the road. But he had something else on his mind, it seemed. He confirmed it in his next statement.

"Lee," he said as I turned to step off the bus, "take one last look at Laramie."

As I looked out the bus window, he said, "God is going to destroy that whole town because of their unwillingness to support this ministry."

I looked at him, amazed that he actually thought God would destroy all those people, as He had destroyed Sodom in the Bible, for a mere money-hungry evangelist. At that moment, I knew beyond a doubt that I was traveling with a preacher who had lost his way.

I told Gene about it when I got settled in the truck. He just shook his head and smiled as he jammed it into gear and guided the rig onto the highway. Donna and the kids pulled out behind us.

Sam passed us not long after we got up to highway speed.

Gene mumbled under his breath as he saw the bus disappear over the next rise. "I told him to take it easy," he said out loud. "He don't have a lick of sense! He'll blow that thing up and expect me to put it back together!"

No more than twenty miles down the road, we heard a pop under the truck and saw a rush of steam behind us. Donna honked her horn and flashed her lights to signal she saw the problem.

Gene pulled over as the truck's heat gauge rose. We got out and tilted the cab forward on the hinges. Donna pulled in behind us.

"We've blown a freeze plug," Gene said as he examined the source of the steam that still gushed from the side of the gas engine. "I'll have to take the car into the next town to get another one."

He got in the Caddy with his family. I sat down beside the truck to wait for their return.

When they returned, they had an extra passenger. As they came to a stop, I could see that it was Sam. He got out of the front passenger seat and silently walked to the front of the truck.

I met Gene at the back of the truck. "What's he doing with you?" I asked.

"He threw a rod in the bus," he answered me. He shook his head and tried to contain his frustration.

I felt that he was about at the end of his patience. I said nothing else but helped him get the tools, and we repaired the truck in silence. Sam stood by looking sheepish, as if he were afraid to speak.

We sat the cab back down on the frame and secured it, and before long we were on the road again. I rode in the car. Sam rode in the truck. I knew he and Gene had some things to sort out.

After reaching the bus, we got everybody fed. I stayed at the bus with the others while Gene and Sam took the truck ahead to find a place to drop off the trailer and return to pull the bus to the same place.

They found a campground in Rock Springs. They also found a truck garage whose owner agreed to let us rent a stall so we could rebuild the engine.

We pulled the bus into the stall and took out the engine. Then we pulled the bus back to the campground so we would all have enough places to sleep.

On the second evening there, Ellen Riley and her daughter drove up. She announced to us that she had decided to go with us and be the secretary. I thought Sam would tell her to go back home, but he welcomed her. It turns out that he had called her and offered her the job. She and her daughter stayed in the bus with Sam and his family. Gene and his family stayed in the trailer. I slept in the Caddy.

After a solid week of work, we had the engine ready to go back in the bus. After another day of installing it, Gene got the honors of starting it. He had a proud and relieved look on his face as it cranked up.

*

Back on the road, Sam sped off again, oblivious to Gene's warning to drive it easy for forty miles or so to loosen the internal engine parts.

We caught up with him at Little America, Wyoming. He said, "This stinkin' thing just ain't runnin' right." Gene listened to it run and decided the engine had

54

jumped time. So we spent another half a day fixing that.

Another few miles down the road, the bus engine locked up completely. We pulled it to the little town of Opal, Wyoming, to spend the night.

We got there just as the only store in town closed up. We caught the guy as he was leaving, and he graciously reopened to let us buy some food for supper. He did not have some kind of milk that Julie needed for their son, and they were hoping they could make it without it.

But as the sun began to set, the boy started having fits. Sam made me go around town knocking on doors asking for this type of milk. I felt like a low-class beggar, not unlike when I was a kid and, after Daddy's injury, we had to get on welfare. I would go with him or Mama to get the government handouts of rice, navy beans, and whatever else they had. Daddy didn't like having to do that, and I took on the same attitude about it.

So knocking on doors for someone else—because they failed to plan in advance—put me in a position I did not like, and it made me mad.

I finally knocked on the door of an elderly couple who had some of the milk. They were kind enough to let me have it.

Chapter Nine

We went on to Idaho and stayed a few days at a KOA campground in Pocatello. While we were there, Sam decided to call his office in Maryland to see if he had gotten any money from anyone. He came back from the phone fighting mad.

"Lee, it seems your parents mailed a certified letter to my office demanding to know where you are. It said if they didn't learn of your whereabouts, they were going to 'take action.' What do you know about that?"

I was in shock. I told him, "Well, I don't know anything about it. I told them in my letter that we were in Laramie."

"You're going to call them and straighten this thing out. Don't tell them where you are now. Tell them you will let them know later. Tell them they had better back off and not cause any trouble."

I did not understand what all the fuss was about. I had told them everyone I had written—my parents, my cousin Mark, my girlfriend, and Curtis—that I was in Laramie. I had given the letters to Sam to pack up and send to his office, just like he had told me to.

He led me to the pay phone and gave me some change. Then he stood nearby so he could listen. I was excited to have the opportunity to call home, but not under these circumstances.

I heard the phone ring, and I could see it in my mind, sitting on the little table against the wall in the kitchen. I heard someone pick it up.

"Hi, Mama."

"Junior?" That was what she had called me all my life, for I was named after my dad. Only when I left for this trip had I had started going by "Lee."

"Yeah, hi, Mama," I repeated.

"Thank God! Junior, are you okay? We have all been worried sick about you. We didn't know if you were still alive, or where you were..."

"I told you where I was in that letter I sent. Didn't you get my letter?" I wondered if the Maryland office had sent out everyone's letters I had written.

"Yes, we got it. But every place you had written about where you were or had been, you or someone had marked out the town and written something else over it. Didn't you get our letters?"

So there it was, I thought. *That's why he had me send them to his "office" in Maryland. He had someone there who censored the letters. That was a dirty trick to play on my parents.*

"No, Mom, I haven't gotten your letters."

"You haven't? Where are you?"

"I can't tell you where we are right now. And, Mama,

the only letter I know about is the certified letter you sent to Maryland, and he is mad about it."

"Who? That man, the preacher? What kind of man is he? What's going on?"

I wished I could tell her. But I did not know. "I will let you know soon. You had better not send any more certified letters, okay? I will let you know more when I can."

Sam, standing close by, nodded his approval at the way I was handling the conversation so far. I wished he would leave so I could say what I wanted to.

"Are you not in Arkansas? That's where that man said you were going."

"No."

"So he lied to us all along?"

"Yes."

I heard her sobbing. "Are you still with him?"

"Yes."

"Are you in danger?"

"No, I'm okay."

"Well, we've been in touch with the highway patrol in several states, but have not had any luck. Wayne was preparing to go look for you, although he did not know where to look. He was going to drive to Arkansas."

Wayne was my youngest sister's husband. He was a Vietnam vet. He had not been in the family very long, but I instantly liked him. *And he was going to take the trouble to try and find me,* I thought. *That's cool of him!*

"I will come home soon. Tell Wayne 'thanks' but I'm okay. I've gotta go now. I'll call back another time."

"Why can't you come home now? We miss you." She started crying hard.

"It's okay, Mama, I'll be home when I can. And don't worry. I'm okay. Tell everyone 'hi' for me."

"Okay. We love you. Call anytime you can. Bye."

"I will. Bye. I love you."

My mind raced as I hung up the phone. It all began to make more sense now. That is why I hadn't gotten a letter from home. If they had written to the Maryland office, which was the only address given, then whoever was censoring my letters would hold theirs, because they would ask specific questions about where I was.

It really bothered me to hear Mama crying. I had seen her hurt a lot in the past several years, and I knew she was hurting now as bad or worse than ever. I felt such pain and anger inside, but I could do nothing to help just yet.

I glared at Sam, who was looking at me, and smiling. Who—what—was this man, and why was he putting my parents through this? I walked past him, and he patted my back. I dodged his touch. I had to get alone and think.

"You did good," he hollered after me. "Real good."

I jerked back around. "Listen, I don't understand this game you're playing, but you have hurt my mom and you're scaring her to death. She doesn't deserve this. I will let her know where we are."

"You will do no such a thing. Not until I say so. You're mine for now, and don't you forget it."

Mumbling under my breath, I climbed into the truck and sat in the dark thinking about the conversation with Mama. I found it hard to understand why someone had changed my letters so that Mama could not tell where I was. What did it matter where we were? I decided to keep my thoughts to myself and not even tell Gene. I was not quite sure how much I could trust him.

I replayed the phone call over and over in my mind. I also thought of the first time that I had tried to talk to Sam. I replayed his abrupt response—"Yeah, what about it?" *Why did I not just walk away then?* I wondered about these things until I fell into a troubled sleep.

*

Sam made some contacts in American Falls, and we held a service at a small church. After the service, a family in the church introduced themselves to us all. They were the Simon family. We went out to eat with them at a local restaurant. John Simon was an upcoming preacher. He seemed real. I immediately felt at ease around him. One family member I was particularly interested in was a girl, about my age, named Jenny. She was John's sister. She did not say much and seemed very shy, but she was a sight for sore eyes. I tried to strike up a conversation with her, but she resisted, so I kept to myself.

Maybe we could become friends, I thought. I remembered Karen back in Laramie and wondered if I wanted to make another friend that I would just have to leave behind.

The following day, Sam took his family in the Caddy to check out another area farther west. He returned a couple of days later, giving us orders to move everything to a campground outside of Declo, Idaho. Then he went back in that direction.

Gene and I headed out the next morning in the truck and trailer. He drove to a big rest stop along

Snake River Canyon. He unhooked the trailer and went back after the bus and his family, leaving me there to watch the trailer. I spent some time walking to the top of the ridge overlooking Snake River. It is a beautiful area, and it felt so peaceful and serene.

It was late afternoon when they returned with the bus. Gene and I roamed the ridge, then went over to the far side of the ridge to climb along the steep cliff. Not being a sure-footed person, I was scared at times that we would fall onto the rocks below. Gene coached me across the sloping mountainside. He was having fun. I was not.

As we were walking back to the bus, he spotted a rabbit. He shot at it with his pistol, but he only stunned it. Then, he sneaked up behind it and hit it with the gun butt. We ate that rabbit for our supper.

We spent the night there, and the next morning I stayed with the trailer again as Gene and Donna pulled the bus on to Declo. Gene came back to get the trailer and me. We headed to the campground to meet the team. It was the fourth of October.

Chapter Ten

We met an elderly couple, Mr. and Mrs. Nay, at the campground. They were staying in a little trailer house in the park and made friends with Sam after seeing the sign on the trailer.

Sam found an old, deserted motel at the intersection of two highways. The motel office was a separate building, at one end of the rooms but closer to the road. An abandoned garage sat in front of the rooms at the other end, at the intersection. Across the highway in front of the motel were railroad tracks. The main part of the town was two blocks beyond the tracks. On the corner across the intersecting highway sat a gas station. The owner of the gas station also managed the motel property. I quickly spotted a pay phone outside the station.

I had my own room at the far end of the row of rooms. I was glad to have the room. Gene and his family had the opposite end. The room nearer to mine was used for storage, and Ellen and Pam stayed in the room nearest Gene's family. Sam and his family stayed on the bus.

We visited a small church in town, called "The Revival Center." The pastor and his wife were very nice. Sam was given a chance to introduce himself in the service. He told about the ministry and spoke of my singing. The pastor's wife asked me to sing in the service, and she liked my performance. After the service, she talked with me.

"Young man," she said, "that was some fine singing. I really felt an anointing when you sang and played."

"Thank you," was my standard answer. I added, "I like to sing for the Lord." As flippant as it may have sounded, I meant what I said. Many times I would feel a peace as I played the piano and sang. It was what I was born to do, and God had arranged the whole thing. We inherited my Grandma's piano when I was ten years old. Mama would play it in the evening after her work was done, and one night I asked her to teach me to play. With a patience beyond my understanding, she worked with me several hours, smiling at my little accomplishments and speaking gently as she showed me how to correct my mistakes. I knew it was God's plan for me to learn when I began to learn it so fast. I began to listen to the radio and pick out on the piano keys what I had heard. I became addicted to learning to play the music I had heard all my life. And Mama's encouragement made it an easier and worthwhile addiction.

The pastor's wife continued, "Is there any way you would have a chance to come sometime during the day and record yourself for me? I have a big recorder. I'll set it up and just leave you alone to play and sing all you want."

"Well, I think I could. I'll see what Sam says we have to do in the next several days. I'll let you know."

I found Sam at the door of the church, and when I

found a place to speak up, I told him of her request.

"Sure," he said enthusiastically. "You can come tomorrow."

I told her I could do it, and we set up a time. She promised to have the recorder set up and ready.

*

I walked the few blocks to the church. The pastor's wife was there as promised, with a reel-to-reel recorder sitting on a cart by the piano. She watched as I played a song, then showed me how to operate the recorder. Then she went back in her house and left me alone to record. I was relieved that she had asked no questions about me, and I volunteered no information. I did not want Sam to suspect that I talked to her about going home.

I enjoyed the time at the piano. I recorded for about an hour, then I sat quietly on the piano bench until she came to check on me and let me go.

As I walked back from the church, I explored the little town. Around the corner from the church was the business part of town. There were various shops and a café. I went into the café and ordered a soda. A few people were there, mainly older couples. Three older men were drinking coffee and discussing whatever old men discuss. Nobody spoke to me, except to take my order. I looked around as I sat at the counter. I spotted a pay phone. I drank my soda and left.

On the road that led back to the motel, I spotted another café across the street on the corner. The outside was a nice brown brick, and it had windows down one side and across the front. The door was cut into the corner of the building. I decided I would check it out another time.

*

The Simon family had arranged for Sam to meet an Indian pastor from the Fort Hall Indian Reservation. They called him "Pastor Jess." Sam, Gene, and I went to meet him at his house on Thursday. He climbed into the Caddy with us and told Sam to drive to a gym on the reservation, between Fort Hall and Blackfoot.

Once we got to the wooden structure, he led us inside to show us where he held weekly church services. There he shared with us his burden as a pastor. He wept as he told us that the American Indians on the reservation had a huge problem with alcohol and drugs. They also were heavy into sniffing paint. A large number of the young Indians on the reservation were already hooked on alcohol and drugs. Several died each year because of overdoses. The addiction to sniffing paint was as bad, and he told us that he personally had found piles of paint cans in places where the young people would meet for "sniffing parties." Many had brain damage because of all of this, and the poverty on the Reservation was worsening because of such misuse of funds and people.

He so passionately shared his burden that I wanted to help in any way I could. I had not witnessed such a heartfelt message in a while, and it really touched me. We all felt the urgency of the situation. He was reaching out for some help in his mission, and asked us to come to his Sunday service. We went that following Sunday night. Sam preached, and before we left, Pastor Jess told us that he had secured permission for us to set up the tent on one of their festival grounds, which was close to the gym.

Chapter Eleven

We moved the equipment trailer to Fort Hall on the 19th of October. Sam borrowed the May's camping trailer, and we parked it a few yards from the tent. The families stayed in Declo at the motel. Gene and I were to take turns sleeping in the tent, but the first few nights we slept in the trailer. I had never slept in one before, so sleeping on the little couch was a neat adventure. Gene made himself at home on the small bed. We sat at the table to eat our meals.

Once again we unloaded the tent, ropes, and stakes. We spent a day setting that all up. The next day we built the stage and set up the folding chairs and tables. We didn't bother with putting sawdust down on the floor as we had in Laramie. On the third day we unloaded and hooked up the equipment.

The restrooms at the ceremonial grounds were outhouses set at the edge of the grounds about two hundred yards behind the tent. At night it seemed like a long trip walking back there in the dark. The coyotes would yelp and scream. Back home I had watched a lot of TV westerns, so as I walked through the dark, I wondered if they were really coyotes. *Maybe it's really Indians*, I would think to myself. It was quite spooky.

The temperature dropped enough at night that we had to use the heater in the camping trailer. Sam bought a propane heater to use in the tent for the services. It was a long, round heater that made a lot of noise. It was so loud when it was running that a person had to speak loudly to be heard around it. We set it at the back of the tent and positioned it to blow heat up the center aisle.

When it came my turn to sleep in the tent, I would normally lie down on the cot on the stage and cover up with mattress pads from the equipment trailer. Sometimes I slept in the center of the tent to get closer to the heater. I would put some chairs together and use mattress pads to lie on and cover up with.

Almost every night some of the young Indians would get drunk and drive around the tent in circles during and after the service, hollering and cussing.

One night after the service I bedded down in the tent on some chairs and was almost asleep when I felt someone looking at me. I opened my eyes, and twenty feet away from me a teenage Indian girl stood motionless, looking straight at me. It startled me to see her there. I sat up and asked if I could help her. She said nothing but walked over to the table at the side of the tent, took some literature, and left the tent.

My heart was still pounding. Then I saw something move out of the corner of my eye. I turned around and saw Gene, who had been in the trailer, step in from the side curtain of the tent. He had his small pistol in his hand. I looked at him, astounded.

"How did you know she was in here?" I asked.

"I heard them pull up. You had that heater in your ear, so you couldn't. There were several of them in the truck. I just wanted to make sure they were not going to cause trouble." He looked out of the curtain. We heard a burst of gravel spewing from the tires as they drove off, laughing loudly.

"Well! I'm glad you heard them. That was a little scary!" I always breathed a little easier when I knew Gene had control.

"Go on to sleep. I'll keep watch from the trailer. I don't think they will be back. They don't mean any harm. Just kids!" He went back out as quickly as he came.

"Wow!" I said to myself. "What a night!" My heart had calmed down enough to lie back down but not enough to let me go to sleep. I pondered for a while about what could have happened, then about seeing Gene holding the pistol at his side, then finally drifted off to dream about bad things.

*

A very curious thing occurred periodically while we were there. Sometimes at night when walking from the tent to the trailer, Gene and I would see blue, eye-shaped lights gliding through the air about twelve inches above the ground. Gene said since we were on the ceremonial grounds, they were probably the spirits of the ancestors hanging out. Under normal circumstances, I would have laughed the theory off, but here Gene had three advantages: For one thing, being an Indian himself, I thought he might know the truth about it. For the second thing, he was hard to read; sometimes he looked very serious when he was joking. I couldn't tell this time if he was joking or not. Thirdly, by now he'd seen me out of so many scrapes with Sam and this whole situation that I would believe just about anything he said!

The second Saturday we were there, Gene drove back to Declo and brought his family back for the final services. I enjoyed being alone. I got hungry and bored, so I took what money I had and walked to the store down the road and bought something to eat. I bought a can of English peas, took them to the trailer, and ate them straight from the can.

Sunday morning, a preacher named Jack Thompson came to the service. He and his wife were about fifty years old. He dressed in cowboy boots and a brown western-cut suit. He had met Sam before the service. He sang a few country gospel songs for us during the service, playing an acoustic guitar he brought with him. I spoke with him after the service, and he gave me a record album of him singing. I thanked him and stuffed it back into my box so it would be safe. I noticed he had written some of the songs on the album.

After the morning service we had a big picnic. People who came to the service brought all kinds of food, and I ate a lot. The Simon family came from American Falls. Jenny was there. We didn't get to visit much, but she was friendlier to me than before. I got her phone number.

On Monday we loaded all the equipment and the stage in the trailer. Tuesday we took the tent down and headed back to Declo.

Chapter Twelve

Back in Declo, I began to feel myself withdrawing from the team. Gene and Sam had their families to visit with, and I didn't want to spend all my time with Gene's family. I sure didn't want to stay in the bus with Sam and his family. It was about two months past time for me to go home, and I knew I should be getting back. I had mailed a few letters, all going through Maryland, but had not heard back from Mama.

I spent a lot of time in my room alone. Gene and Sam began buying and selling cars to make some money to operate on, and they were gone to Burley a lot. Although I went with them some, I was content to stay in seclusion. Besides, I had to figure out the best time to call home.

The Simons came to Declo a couple of times to see us. Once they brought us some elk meat. It had a wild taste, and I did not like it very much. I ate it because I was hungry. But I thought it was interesting to have the opportunity to eat elk.

Jenny was talking to me a little more on their visits, so one evening I decided I would try to call her. I figured I would go to the café where I had seen the pay phone. I left the motel when Sam and Gene were gone and went to the café. I dialed the operator and told her the number to call. As I was waiting for the call to go through, I saw the Caddy pass slowly by the café. A minute later, Sam came in. The look on his face reminded me of the look my daddy had on his face when he caught me smoking in a little café after school.

"Are you trying to call your folks?" He spoke in low tones so no one else could hear.

"No. I'm calling Jenny."

He sneered at me. "I don't think you are. I think you are sneaking off to call your folks. Get back to the motel. I'll meet you there in ten minutes." With that, he turned around, spoke to the guy behind the counter, and walked out.

I walked slowly back to the motel. *He actually did not believe I was calling Jenny,* I thought. *He just called me a liar!*

When I got back to the motel, he was standing in the door of the bus. I walked past the bus, barely looking up and not saying a word. I went to my room, cleaned up, and went to bed.

The next evening while Sam and Gene were gone to Burley, I decided I *would* call my parents. I went to gas station across the street to use the open pay phone by the curb. While the operator was connecting me with home, I saw the Caddy. Gene was driving. They pulled up to the curb by me and came to a screeching halt. I shuddered. Sam motioned me to the car.

"Get over here," he hollered.

I hung the up receiver and slowly walked to the car.

"Who were you calling? Your folks?"

I looked down at the asphalt, saying nothing.

"I asked you a question."

I looked him in the eye and said, "I'm calling my mom." I was so mad I was shaking.

"Get in the car."

"I'm calling my mom," I repeated.

"You're doing what I tell you to do."

I glared at him for a long minute. Then I slowly climbed into the back seat, afraid that if I pressed on, I probably wouldn't live long enough to call home. There would be another time.

*

I found that time a couple of days later, when the two of them were gone to Burley again on business. This time I got through without interruption.

It was Daddy who answered the call. I heard him repeat my name when the operator asked if he would accept a call from me.

"Hello."

"Hi, Daddy."

"Son?" His voice cracked as he said it. He started weeping.

"Yeah, it's me," I said, somewhat touched by his emotion. I tried hard, but there was too much anger built up inside for me to want to talk to him much.

"Son, I'm glad you called. Your mother cries herself to sleep every night. Her pillow stays soaked, and she's worryin' herself sick about you." He sounded truly concerned about Mama.

"Well, is she there? Let me talk to her."

"Okay." I heard him tell Mama I was on the phone. I heard her gasp and grab the phone.

"Hi, Son!" Her voice was quivering.

"Hi, Mom," I said.

"Are you okay? Where are you? Can you tell me?"

"I'm in Declo, Idaho, now. He don't know I'm calling."

"Idaho? Oh, my goodness! We thought you were in Arkansas. That's where that man said you were going. So you went from Arkansas to Idaho?"

"No. Actually, we didn't go to Arkansas. We went straight to Wyoming. Laramie, Wyoming. That's what I wrote in the letters."

"Well, we didn't know, because that was all marked through..."

"Yeah, I know. You told me when I called you from Pocatello."

After a short silence, Mama said, sternly, "So he lied to us all along?"

"Yes."

"Are you still with him?"

"Yes."

"Well, okay. I'm glad to know where you are. What was the name of the town?"

"Declo, Idaho." She repeated it back and wrote it down.

"Okay, Mama, I'll be home when I can. And don't worry. I'm okay. Tell everyone 'hi' for me."

"Okay. We love you, Son. Call soon if you can."

"I will. I love you, too. Miss you. See you soon. Bye."

"B...bye." I heard her sobbing as she hung up the phone. In my mind's eye, I could see her head dip almost to the little table the phone sat on, holding the receiver to her ear as long as she could before she could let herself let go.

I was furious. I would confront Sam about this. First, I had to cool off. I had to think. I walked uptown to the café I had spotted with all the windows. There I could spot Gene and Sam if they came hunting me.

*

It was almost dark when I got to the café. Through the window in the front door I could see a group of teenagers sitting inside around a big table and others around a pool table. I hesitated and almost turned around to leave. But they all seemed to be having a good time, and I felt a twinge of hope for a chance to meet someone my own age. I walked on in and went to the counter to order a soft drink.

"Hello, young man," the waiter behind the counter said cheerfully. "What will it be for you today?"

"Well, do you have R.C.?" It was my favorite.

"Yes, I do. One R.C. comin' up."

I looked around as he loaded up a red plastic glass with ice and poured my drink over it.

"Thanks," I said, glad to be waited on. I walked to a table and looked at the teenagers as I went by them. Three or four of them looked at me as I passed by, and one boy spoke to me faintly—like you do when you don't want to appear to be a snob but you don't necessarily want to engage in conversation. I understood the gesture and honored his kindness by responding with a "hi" as I passed. I sat down at a table several feet away, where I got lost in my thoughts about the conversation with Mama.

I still could not get over the fact that Sam had censored my letters. *I no longer have respect for Sam at all,* I decided. *But I will still have to be civilized to him and everyone else just to survive until I can get away. I don't know why it has to be this way.*

I told Mama I would be home as soon as I can. How do I hope to do that? The truth is, I am trapped and can't see my way out of this. How am I supposed to get home? I have no money, and I can't ask my family for any. They live week to week and can't afford to send me money. All of my sisters live the same way. Cousin Mark had understood when I was in danger at home, and would drive the three hours from Dallas to Abilene to visit or pick me up anytime I called him. But I am clear across the country now. I can't call and ask him to help me here. No one can help. I got myself into this, and I will get myself out.

I have no way of making extra money. I know Gene is getting a little more money from Sam than I am, and rightfully so. He has a family to support. At least he has options. He has been making a little money on automobiles he and Sam are buying and selling. But I know he is just getting by. I was not asked to join their sales ventures. That is okay with me. But I am still scraping pennies...

I heard the teenagers laughing, and it brought me back to my surroundings. I looked around, and they still seemed to be having a good time. Some were still playing pool, and some were playing pinball. It reminded me of my friends in the youth group back home. Some of the best times I had experienced before I left home had been with the youth group at our church. We would go eat pizza and have a lot of fun together. I missed them. I also missed my friend Curtis. *I should try to call him. Maybe he could tell me what to do. He was always good with advice.*

I looked over the group of teenagers there. Maybe if I could talk to them and get to know them, they could be my friends. Maybe they would listen to my story and understand how I felt. But they probably wouldn't. They seemed like a close group. They were at home. They all had their families and probably would not like an outsider. Besides, we would be leaving Declo soon anyway.

No one at the teen's table had made an attempt to start a conversation, and neither did I. I finished my drink and went back to the motel.

Chapter Thirteen

The following morning, I decided to confront Sam with my thoughts. One thing about my experiences at home in the previous couple of years was that I learned that sometimes a person just *has to* face the enemy to keep from getting trampled on. I went to the motel office where Sam and the secretary were figuring the cash situation.

"Hi, Lee," he said, glancing up from the desk as I entered. He seemed to be in a friendly mood.

"Hey," I said casually. I sat down in a chair and looked out the window for a long minute. When I had my nerve, I spoke calmly. "I called my parents last night." I waited for his response. There was none. It was as if he already knew it or suspected it.

I continued, "Mama has been worried sick about me, because until I told her last night, she didn't know where I am. You know you had no right to censor my letters." I paused and watched him.

Now I had his attention. His face turned red, and he got up from the desk and faced me. I took a quick look at Ellen. She was standing on the far side of the desk, looking scared. Her eyes following the preacher as he walked slowly toward me. For once I was glad she was around.

"You should not have called home," he growled. "I am very disappointed."

"I don't care if you are disappointed!" I snapped back. "You've disappointed me, too! I came with you to make some money—seventy-five dollars a week. That's what you said. Ain't it?"

"I can't pay you," he retorted. "I don't have the money. You have to wait like everybody else to get paid. Now get out of here. We have work to do." He stared at me angrily.

I stood up. "Well, if you don't start paying me, I'm going to leave."

I had said it without thinking.

He grinned suddenly. "Leave, then! Where ya going? You going to hitchhike?"

I had no answer. I went out and slammed the door behind me. I went to Gene's room to tell him about the whole thing. He saw I was upset and led me outside. He stood against the back of the motel as I told him about the phone call to Mama and about confronting Sam. He was quiet for a minute. He seemed to think things out and analyze situations before acting on them.

After a long silence, I said, "Gene, did you know he censored my letters?"

"No. I knew he sent them to Maryland, but I didn't know why."

"It makes me so mad. I just want to leave. I have no place to go. I don't have the money to get home. I don't have anyone up here—except you, of course. I don't know what to do."

"Just stay here with us. We'll figure something out. I'm not getting paid that much either."

He invited me to eat breakfast with them. Donna had made some chocolate biscuits and chocolate gravy. I had never heard of such a thing before this trip. They were tasty, and I learned to like them quickly. Much of the time I ate in the bus with Sam's family, but I didn't want to go near it this morning.

Gene was quiet as he ate. He didn't tell Donna about what I had told him. "I'll tell you what we will do, Lee," he said. "You and I will go to the post office and see if we can get mail delivered 'general delivery.' Then when you call your folks back, you can tell them to send mail here. Sam won't know we are doing it."

"Okay. That will be good."

After I ate, I went back to my room and wrote Mama a letter. This time I'd send it on my own. I told them some about where we had been and the mountains I'd seen. And I wrote about Snake River. I wanted her and the rest of the family to know I was enjoying myself at least some of the time.

That evening, the Simons came to visit. We all went to Burley to eat supper at a restaurant. I guess it was Sam's way of trying to relieve everyone's tension. On the way in, I spotted a pay phone. After everyone was seated, I decided to call Mama and tell her what I had written in the letter that morning.

Mama answered the phone. What she told me chilled me to the bone. I hung up and stomped to the table.

Standing over Sam, I said, "I just called home again. Mama said you called today. She said you told them you were adopting me and they'd never see me again. You lying creep! How could you do that to my parents?"

Sam was on his feet and grabbing my arm as I finished. Everyone else sat quietly. He pulled me out front of the restaurant.

"Don't you ever do that again. You embarrassed me in front of the whole place. Don't you know people will see us, and they know who I am? You'll ruin everything for us here. Yes, I called your folks. And I told them they'd never see you again. And if you keep this up, they won't! I am going to adopt you. I want you to stay with me."

"I will not let you do that. I hate you. You're crazy! You don't even like me. I want to go home."

"No. You cannot go home. You're staying with me." With that, he walked back into the restaurant.

I was baffled. I didn't know what else to do. I went back in and sat there with the rest of them, but I couldn't eat.

I said nothing else to him that night. After returning to Declo, I went to my room, but I couldn't sleep. A struggle was going on in my head, and I could not settle it down. I sat in the dark in a chair, leaning back against the wall. *Think,* I told myself.

Later, after it seemed everyone had gone to bed, I opened the door of my room and looked out. I heard and saw no movement. I quietly stepped out and walked to the front of the motel, past the office, and to the edge of the highway. I stood in the dark thinking about what I had seen since I left home: beautiful scenery like I had never seen in my life, mountains and rivers I never knew existed. The day alone at Snake River Canyon was a treat. It was so peaceful there looking down at the water. I didn't mind being alone there.

But I knew I was not really alone there, because God was there. He was in the wind that blew across the water and the grass up on the mountain. He was with me at the Indian reservation. There my imagination had gone wild, thinking about Indians and the Western movies I had seen. The nights sleeping in the camping trailer were nice. Those mysterious blue lights moving alone the ground and the night I had been awakened by the feeling of someone staring at me—though scary at the time, both were neat experiences to reflect on. None of what I had been through and seen had escaped Him.

Though I felt alone in the dark nights in Declo, I knew I was not really alone there either. I thought of Mama at home, on her knees in that center bedroom praying for me. I knew she was praying. I had heard her too many times in my life to think she would stop now. I knew she was hurting, too, missing her only son and wondering if I was truly okay.

I knew I had to get home. I had no idea how to do it. I was in a hard place. I was afraid of what Sam might do if I left. If he had someone in Maryland, he might have someone in Abilene. Somehow he had made enough contacts while he was in Abilene to gather a bunch of food donations. Maybe he still had someone there working for him, someone he could call to harass or hurt my family. I couldn't chance that. I was tired of him, and I didn't trust him as far as I could throw the bus. But did I really want to go back to the life I had come from at home?

Although I did miss Mama, my friends, and the church folks, I knew that life at home was hard. It was a tough decision to make. Even if I had the chance to get away, how could I?

So what should I do—here and now? I thought. *Should I just grab my things and walk out tonight? The road is empty as far as I can see. But surely someone will come by and pick me up before daylight.*

But where would they take me? Not all the way to Texas, I know. And how could I trust a complete stranger driving down the highway? Maybe they would be honest and try to help me; maybe they wouldn't. That would be a stupid gamble, I decided. *That's how I got to this point—trusting strangers. If I leave, I could find myself in a worse situation than I am already in. If there is anything I don't need, it's to be picked up and murdered. Mama would never know where I ended up. A morbid thought, but it could happen.*

Deciding against taking such a chance, I walked back to my room and fell asleep wondering what the next day would bring. I felt helpless.

Chapter Fourteen

Pastor Jess sent word through the Simons that he wanted us to minister at a Sunday evening service as soon as possible. So we made arrangements to go the following Saturday to talk to him and see what instruments we would need to bring.

"We'll be in the same gym as before," he told us. I knew there was an old PA set, a piano that I could play, and a small drum set. So we would just need guitars and an amp for Gene, a microphone and stand for me. *Good,* I thought. *Less work!*

Jess's son, Robert, drove up to the gym in a roar while we were practicing before service. He was a friendly guy. He came in with two young friends on his heels. He shook our hands and introduced his friends.

"What kind of tank are you driving?" Gene teased. "We heard you blaze in here!"

"It's a Plymouth Barracuda. It's fast!" he exclaimed, smiling.

"A Barracuda?" Gene responded. "What year?"

"It's a '65," came the response.

"Let's see it." I noticed Gene seemed genuinely interested.

We followed him out to look at it. It was painted black but had a brown hood and no windshield. It had worn-out mud grips on the back. A big back window sloped gently to a stubby trunk lid. Inside, it had a floor shift and a four-speed standard transmission.

"I wrecked it," Robert explained. "I replaced the hood but have not found a windshield for it. I'm gong to sell it soon."

Gene drove it around a dirt baseball diamond beside the gym. It was a wild ride, sliding sideways almost all the way.

"You want to sell it now?" Gene asked.

"Yeah, sure," the boy answered.

"Okay. If the price is right, I'll bring you the money this week."

They talked about the price, and Gene committed to purchasing the car real soon.

As promised, he bought it that very week. He found a windshield in Burley, and we put it in. He let me drive it some for helping him. I liked the car. It was not a big car. It seemed just my size.

*

Back in Declo, Sam told us our next destination would be Meridian, Idaho. A suburb of Boise, Meridian was almost two hundred miles west of Declo. He had gone there to scout out prospects for the winter months and found an old empty theater building that was for rent.

Gene and I had instructions to take the 'Cuda and the camping trailer, park on the empty lot adjacent to the theater, and wait for Sam to show up.

We headed out about noon on Saturday, November 4. The trip up the interstate highway was a treat, a nice road with beautiful mountain scenery in the distance.

But every trip we took lately had become an adventure with its own surprises. This one was no exception. We ran out of gas about twenty miles from Boise. The 'Cuda was using a lot of it pulling the trailer. Gene stayed in the car while I walked about a mile to a gas station. I was glad I was accustomed to walking across town back home to see friends and to go to school, because I made it to the gas station easily. The station attendant let me use a gas can for a small deposit.

I headed back to the car, and a truck driver stopped beside me, reached across to open the passenger door, and motioned for me to get in. As I climbed into the big Freightliner, I saw the big dash wrapped around the driver to the center of the cab, with all kinds of buttons and knobs. I was amazed at the difference between this big rig and the small cab-over GMC we traveled in. We introduced ourselves, and I told him where I was headed as we traveled the sort distance to the car. The big truck and the kindness of the driver eased my nerves. I thanked him as I got out, and I walked across the highway to the car. Gene poured the gas in the tank. He saved a little of the gas to prime the carburetor, and I cranked the starter until the engine roared to life again.

*

Meridian seemed like a nice small town, although it was bigger and busier than Declo. We drove to the downtown area on Main Street and found the theater, half a block down a side street with an empty lot between it and a store on the corner that faced Main Street. The theater was a freestanding building made of cinder blocks, brick, and stucco. The name on the marquee proudly proclaimed "Roxy Theater."

We parked the car and trailer on the empty lot and got out to have a look around.

"Well, let's check it out," Gene said as we walked around to the front of the theater.

I had never been allowed to go into a theater. Mama was real strict about that. It was one thing I had not disobeyed. Now I was naturally curious about how it looked.

Glass cases were imbedded into the front stucco walls to display the movie posters. The walls gave way to a two-door entrance. I peered through the locked doors to get a glimpse inside, but it was too dark to see much beyond the first few feet of carpet.

I surveyed the neighborhood around the theater. Although we were downtown, it seemed like a quiet area. Facing the street, Main Street was to my left at the end of the block. On the opposite corner of the road stood a five-and-dime store with big display windows across the front. More stores and shops lined the sidewalk, beside that store and across from the Roxy. To my right, between the theater and the corner, were two old houses with big trees in the front yards. Opposite the houses, on the corner, stood a small brick fire station. Concrete steps led up to the door.

We went back to the trailer to disconnect it from the 'Cuda and set it up for our stay.

Sunday was a lazy day. Gene bought a local paper and began looking up places for the families to move into. We drove around town to check out the town and went to the grocery store for supplies.

Sam showed up about midday Monday in the Caddy. He had called the realtor before joining us, and the realtor came quickly with the key. He unlocked the theater, took us for a quick tour, and produced a rental contract for Sam to sign. Then he was gone.

We took our own tour through the building. Inside, a foyer with red, tan, and blue carpet and a ticket booth welcomed us. It was still as inviting as it must have been for many years. On the right, an open door past the ticket booth and snack counter revealed an office. On the left were two rest rooms and a staircase beyond a closed rust-colored wooden door. We went through one of the doors in a wall separating the foyer from the auditorium. The auditorium remained intact, with theater seats divided by two aisles. It was smaller than what I had imagined a theater auditorium to be. The screen still stood ready for service on the stage. Big curtains on each side of the stage gave the old building a grand feeling.

"The first thing we'll do," Sam said, "is tear out the screen."

I looked up at the massive screen, which reached almost to the ceiling above the stage. There was not a tear in it. *That will be such a waste*, I thought. Then I asked, "Are you sure we can do that? We won't get in trouble?"

"Yes, we can do that," Sam mocked. "And we're going to. Then, Gene, you'll need to find the electrical outlets and run some extension cords for us to hook the instruments into."

"No problem," Gene said.

We went through a door on the left side of the stage and entered a room with a door that opened to the alley and another door that led to two more rooms behind the stage. On a shelf in the first room were several piles of movie fliers, the type to be displayed behind the glass panels on the front of the theater to advertise what movies are playing. Full-color posters of great movies such as *Gone with the Wind* and *West Side Story* were among the seemingly endless piles. A pile of coal lay on the floor in front of the shelf and under a wooden windowpane housing a metal door. The innermost room held the heat source for the theater, a coal stoker and furnace.

"You'll have to learn how to do this, Lee," Sam said. "Keeping the theater heated up will be your responsibility. You'll stay here, keep the place clean, and keep it warm. We'll have to get some more coal soon. Gene, you ever work one of these?"

I threw Gene a glance, which he correctly interpreted as a plea for help. I had never seen—or even heard of—a furnace like it.

"No, but Lee and I will figure it out," he answered. "We have a few days."

"Okay, then. I'll leave it with you."

We walked back to the front of the building. Sam was spurting out orders to Gene, and I knew we were in for some work. "Let's get some tools, and I'll help you guys tear the screen down." He sounded almost jubilant about it.

After we tore down the screen with hammers and screwdrivers, we piled it outside at the alley for the trash men to discard. Sam dusted off his clothes and announced that he would return to Declo to prepare the rest of the group to come to Meridian. He would be back in a couple of days.

"When you get finished cleaning the auditorium and office and figure out that furnace, you'll go to Declo and bring the truck and trailer. Then we'll pull the bus up here. I'll have to find a place to park it so Julie, the kids, and me can stay in it. Buy a paper and look for a place for your family, Gene. Ellen and Pam can stay in the camping trailer. I'll see you later."

Then he left for Declo.

Gene and I looked at one another. It was late afternoon, and there was a lot to be done. We walked through the theater again, rehearsing things we had to do.

"Let's go buy some rags, brooms, and mops. We'll get started early in the morning. Hey, let's check out the upstairs," he said, pointing to the doorway in the foyer. "That may be where you sleep."

We walked up the stairs into a big room. Two old movie projectors stood on their pedestals on the inside wall of the room, complete with the empty film reels that had, in a distant past, held a host of movies. Between the projectors, a window looked over the auditorium. Further around the room were a couple of fold-up chairs and a desk. On the wall by the stairs hung a wash basin. A small door beside it went to a rest room. On the outside wall, a door opened to a long, narrow balcony over the marquee. The walls were in need of paint, smoky from the years of burning coal in the furnace that was ducted through the old building.

"This will be the warmest room for you to stay in. The furnace will heat this room up faster since it's higher and smaller. We'll get the cot out of the trailer for you to sleep on. It's not the best in the world, but at least it beats nothing."

Later, we found a store where we could buy some food and cleaning supplies. Then we returned to the little trailer for some supper and rest.

Chapter Fifteen

On Tuesday morning, I slept in a little later than usual and stirred only when I smelled coffee. Gene was sitting at the table reading a newspaper. Breakfast was a box of doughnuts. We took our time getting around.

We stepped out of the trailer into a cold winter morning and decided we needed to light the furnace in the theater before we could clean. Looking it over and flipping a switch on the wall, Gene said, "Oh, yeah, we'll have this going in no time."

"Good," I shivered. "I can't take this much cold."

He found a shovel in the pile of coal that lay on the floor in the adjacent room and filled up the stoker. He then turned on the switch. The stoker made a grinding noise. The coal started churning in the hopper, and the big auger at the bottom of it started moving the coal toward the furnace.

"The idea here is that the furnace will continue to burn if coal is kept in the stoker. All you have to do is fill up the hopper, turn on the auger switch, put some

93

kindling in the furnace under the coal in there, light it with a match, wait for the coal to fire up, and turn on the blower switch. The heat blows through the building vents to heat up the entire theater."

"What kindling?" I asked.

He directed me to the movie posters in the other room. "These."

I protested, thinking that would be a waste of good posters, but that did not change his mind.

"That's why they are in here, Lee," he said.

We walked to the far side of the furnace, opened the door, and stuffed some movie fliers into it. Then he lit the paper with a match. After a few minutes, the coal began to burn. He turned on the blower switch. The noise in the room was deafening, with the stoker grinding, the fire burning, and the blower blowing. He motioned for me to follow him back into the auditorium.

"We'll see how long it takes to heat this place. Let's go to the projector room first." We went up into the projector room and prepared it for me to sleep in.

After a couple of hours, it began to feel not as cold in the center of the auditorium, and we began to dust off the seats.

Later that day, Gene went to get some electrical connections to complete the wiring runs for the instruments. I had his portable radio playing in the auditorium as I mopped the uncarpeted sections of flooring under the seats. I was about half through with the right side of the seating when I heard a female voice behind me say, "Hi."

I whirled around because it startled me, not knowing anyone was there. There stood two teenaged girls, smiling at me, holding schoolbooks. One was a pretty, pleasant-looking blonde, about my height. The other was an equally pretty redhead, a little shorter.

"Hi," I replied. I reached to turn the radio down.

"What are you guys doing here?" the blonde asked. "Are you going to reopen the theater?"

"No. We're opening a revival center."

"Revival center? What's that?"

"It's a church. We're going to have church in here for a while."

"Why?" The blonde looked at me curiously.

"Well, we travel around holding church services. We normally set up a big tent in towns, but it's too cold this time of year, so we rented the theater for services here. It's just to get people in church, started on the right road."

"On the right road?" The redhead was clearly not a churchgoer.

"Yeah," I tried to explain, "you know, saved by Jesus. Going to heaven. Living right."

"Okay." The redhead was apparently tired of this conversation. "How old are you?"

"I'm sixteen," I said, knowing I looked older.

"I'm Dorie," said the blonde. She smiled at me and seemed pleased to hear my age. "She's Sue."

"Hi, Dorie and Sue. I'm Lee," I said. "Nice to meet both of you."

"Well, we've got to go."

"Okay. Y'all stop and visit anytime, and come to the services if you'd like. I'll be playing the organ up there." I pointed to the empty stage.

"Okay. See you," Dorie said, waving as she walked backwards up the aisle. Sue spun her around, and I heard them giggle as they walked into the foyer of the building and out the door.

"Well," I said to myself, "this might be an interesting stay after all!"

*

Late Thursday morning we finished cleaning and were ready for the instruments, so we headed for Declo. Gene was ready to see his family, and he pushed the 'Cuda a little. It was a fun car to ride in. I decided I would like to have it. I knew Gene would not keep it long. I wondered if I might have a chance at buying it. I brought up the subject.

"Gene, I think this would make me a great car. I like it. When you decide to sell it, I want first crack at it, if Sam pays me right in Meridian. What do you think you'll want for it?"

Gene took his eyes off the road long enough to throw me a glance. "Oh, I don't know. Maybe we could work out somethin'." He smiled behind his cigarette.

Realizing that he was not going to give me anything more definite at the moment, I turned the conversation toward a more interesting subject. "You know those two girls I told you about yesterday? The ones who stopped by while I was mopping."

He smiled at me again, like he knew what I was thinking. "Yeah, you told me. What about them?"

"Well, I sure hope they come back to see me. They were nice to talk to. And a whole lot prettier than you to look at!"

We both laughed about it, and Gene got quiet. I knew his mind went back to thinking about his family he was on the way to see. I thought about my family that I was so far away from and wondered when I would see them again.

It wouldn't be any time soon, if Sam had his way. I knew that for a fact. Every time I'd say something about going home, he would sneer and say, "Just how are you getting there?" I didn't know, so I would drop the subject.

Yeah, I sure hope them girls come back, I thought as I watched the scenery zip by.

*

At Declo, we visited the crew and ate a late lunch in the bus. Then I went to my room, lay across the bed, and started another letter to my mom. I spent most of the afternoon there, enjoying the quiet seclusion of the old gray walls. I fell asleep.

Bang, bang, bang! Someone was beating on my door and telling me to come to supper. I stirred from my dreams and said I'd be right there. I washed my face in the little bathroom sink and headed out the door, wondering what Julie had cooked up in the bus. I was surprised to find out that Gene and Donna had cooked for everyone and we were to have supper in their room.

After the meal, Gene and I loaded up supplies in the trailer. Then we were headed back to Meridian.

We spent Friday running wires and getting the instruments ready for the service. I practiced up on the organ, ready to sing my songs for a new batch of people—and for two pretty girls, I hoped.

Sam drove back up that day to see how things were going and to pick up Gene and the truck so they could pull the bus up there. He slept in the camping trailer with Gene that night.

"You might as well sleep in the theater starting tonight so the trailer won't be so crowded," Gene told me. "You need to get used to it anyway."

"Fine with me," I answered. I was glad to not stay in the same place as Sam. I had already set a cot up in the projector room. I had taken furniture covers from the trailer for a pad under me and for my cover. I took my box of clothes with me and climbed the stairs. I arranged things the way I wanted them. Then I looked through the window into the auditorium. The place looked big and lonely. I went down the stairs to check the door and turn out the lights. Finally, I lay down on the cot, thought of home, and fell asleep.

Chapter Sixteen

I woke up and slowly turned over on the cot. My back was stiff—too stiff for a sixteen year old. Something was wrong. I smelled smoke. I sat up on the edge of the cot. Even in the darkness, I realized I was surrounded by smoke. I figured out that the fire in the furnace had gone out and the blower was blowing the smoke through the building's air ducts.

I got up and made my way to the light switch. The smoke was so thick that the light hardly made a difference. I had to feel my way down the stairs, turning lights on as I went through foyer, the auditorium, and into the rooms behind the stage.

Once there, I turned on the light and shut off the switches for both the blower and the stoker. The smoke was not as thick there; it had been blown through the ducts. I checked to see how much coal was left in the stoker, filled it up with some of the coal piled on the floor, crinkled up some of the old movie posters, and stuffed them in the furnace. I then struck a match and lit the papers. I stood there and watched until the coal caught fire. I turned on the stoker and the blower and watched it a while longer until I was quite sure it would burn through the night. Then I walked back to the front of the building and opened the front door to clear the smoke out.

I decided not to bother the guys about the smoke. I had already taken care of it. I was a little proud that I handled it as well as I did. Then I got a folding chair and my coat from my room and sat against the front wall under the marquee so I could get some fresh air and think things over.

I could have been killed in there! Then what would Mama have done? And how would I have felt—providing I had lived long enough to think about it—knowing that I had asked to go on a trip that had gotten me killed? I heard myself chuckling about thinking that way, and I realized how sleepy I was.

I glanced at the fire station at the end of the block and, for a moment, contemplated going there to see if they could help me get home. There was no movement around it that I could see. I figured the firemen were asleep in there; they never showed up to see what all the smoke was about. *It's just as well,* I thought.

I got up to see if the smoke had cleared enough for me to close the doors and go back to bed. It had, so I locked the front doors and climbed the stairs.

*

Saturday morning came too early. I woke up with Gene knocking on the projector room door.

"Lee," he said, "it's time to get up. We're leaving for Declo."

"This early?" I asked.

"Yeah, we want to get there early so that if we have trouble we can still get back before dark. Sam says you can stay or go. It's really up to you."

I thought a minute about it. I could go back and see my little room there and maybe go back to the café for a soda. Or I could stay in Meridian and have some time to look around the area at my leisure. And maybe Dorie would come by.

"I'll stay here, if you're sure you don't need me."

"Nope! We will be okay. You take the day off." Gene smiled at me as if he knew I needed some time to myself. I think he envied me a little for my youth and the little bit of freedom I seemed to find in the most unlikely places.

After they left, I took a chair outside and sat under the marquee. It was not as cold as the day before, and the sun warmed me up just enough to enjoy the morning.

Later, I decided to explore the next block across Main. I found a pay phone mounted on the front wall of a café. I was glad to find it, because I knew I needed to call home again. I wanted to stay in touch.

I called in the afternoon. Daddy answered, and he had the same story as before. He said Mama cried herself to sleep every night, and her pillow would be wet with tears. She wanted me home. When he gave the phone to Mama, she told me that Daddy had stopped drinking so much, and she just knew things would be better for us if I came back home. I said I would be home soon, said, "Good-bye—and pray for me," and hung up. I wondered if my absence had brought them closer together. *That would make the trip worth the trouble,* I thought to myself.

Gene and Sam came back without the bus. Gene said the owner had it locked it up with a chain and was going to keep it locked up until he got paid what he was owed. Sam was fit to be tied. I stayed out of his way and tried to do my duties with no trouble. He found a motel for his family and rented a trailer in a small trailer park outside of town for Gene and his family. They found a spot in the same trailer court for the Nay's small camping trailer that Ellen and Pam would stay in.

Sunday, they took the two cars back to Declo to bring everyone back. I stayed at the theater and practiced on the organ.

Late that same evening, Sam was in his office at the theater. I knocked on the door.

I saw him through the window as he looked up from his Bible. "Come in," he said.

I opened the door and walked in. I was hoping he would be in a receptive mood. I sat in the chair in front of the small desk.

"What's on your mind?" he asked.

"I want to go home. I need to go home. My mother is not doing too well with me gone. Daddy says she cries all the time. I don't care if I have to come back. I just have to go."

Sam looked at me like he actually felt my pain. "Well," he said slowly, "we're about to start services here, and I can't do it without you. I'll tell you what: you stay with me through the next two weeks, and I'll buy you a bus ticket so you can go home for a couple of weeks. Then you come back, and we'll see what is in the works then. Will you agree to that?"

I nodded my head, wanting to believe he would really let me go. "Okay," I said. "I'll agree to that. I'll stay for the services; then I'll go home and make sure everyone's all right. Thank you. That's cool!"

I walked out of the office feeling good about having a calm conversation with him. I also walked out with more hope of going home than I had felt in months.

Chapter Seventeen

As promised, the services began the following Monday evening, the 13th of November. We would not have day services, Sam explained, because the people probably would not come out that much in the cold weather. That was great with me!

The theater looked empty at the Monday night service. Not many people came, although Sam had made fliers and posted them in businesses around town. He also put an ad in the paper.

After the service, I wrote a short letter to Mama on a postcard. I tried to think of something I had not talked about. I remembered hearing some news on the radio. I thought it would impress them knowing I had paid attention, so I wrote:

Mom,

It looks like Nixon got elected again! Bull!
I will be home in about a week and a half. I'll

play here for another week and be home three days afterward.

When I get home, I want to go to each of my sisters' houses for about a week. Okay?

How do you like the picture on this card? If my plans go right, I'll be able to bring you and Dad up here sometime and stay a while.

Well, I'll go for now.

Bye. God bless you.

Lee

I knew Sam had said I could be home for two weeks, but I was feeling bold enough to think about staying longer out of his grip. Besides, I felt like I had to give Mama some kind of encouragement that things could get back to normal. I also wanted to see my sisters. I was hoping that would work out.

*

Tuesday night I noticed a bigger crowd coming into the theater. I felt confident about my work on the organ, and pretended they had heard about my performing and had all come to hear me.

From the stage, I spotted a lady in the audience concentrating on Gene and I. She was in her thirties, I guessed. She had a long dress on, which set her apart from most of the congregation. And she had a peculiar stare as she watched us play. I threw Gene a glance between songs and tipped my head her direction. He nodded that he had noticed, and smiled. I saw her talking to Sam after the service, and listened in. Seems she played an accordion and wanted to sit in with us on stage. Sam politely said no.

Also there that night was a young preacher, Billy, and his wife, Sherry. After the service dismissed, they introduced themselves to us. We all sat in the back of the auditorium as they shared their vision. They were from Boise and were very involved in youth ministry. They were looking for a building to rent for a youth center and were hoping to use the Roxy along with us until they could get one. I liked them immediately, and they were nice to me.

The accordion lady came back on Wednesday night. She introduced herself to me before I could get to the stage. Her name was Janet.

"I really like the way you play," she said.

"Thank you," I replied, smiling. I meant it, too. No matter what I thought about a person, I was glad when they recognized the talent I had.

"I would like to play along sometime."

I think Sam said no, I thought. "Well, I'll see what I can do." I really had no intention of asking about it. I did not like pushy people.

Dorie and Sue came on Thursday night. I spotted them after the first song. I could not keep from smiling as I saw Dorie looking at me and waving when she saw me look at her. We talked for a few minutes after the service, and they said they would be back.

"You play and sing pretty good," Dorie said to me.

"Thanks," I said. I really liked *her* telling me!

*

Friday we had about eighty in attendance. After the service our new preacher friend, Billy, asked me if I would like him to pick me up Saturday to spend some time with himself and Sherry. I said that would be great. The arrangements were made with Sam, and I was glad to have plans for something different to do.

Saturday morning, Gene and Sam came in together. Gene handed me a sandwich. He and Sam were talking about selling cars.

"We'll look in the newspaper and find some we can buy at a good price, and see if we can make a profit on them. We have to watch it, though, and not waste any money. We have to buy them cheap."

"Okay," Gene replied. "I'll get a paper tonight and see if there are any in there that we can get quick."

"All right." Sam seemed satisfied. "I have another idea, too. I'm going to call some grocery stores to see if we can get them to donate to a charity for underprivileged families—like we did in Abilene. I think we're going to stay here through Christmas. I may call some clothing stores, and I'll try to get some toys for the kids. I'll register a charity under 'The Lord's Army' name." He gave me a smug look. "I will put an ad in the paper in case individuals want to donate, too. That will work out fine. We will use Billy's VW van to go around to pick up the goods. We will put everything in the foyer of the theater. I'll talk to Brother Billy."

Just listening to his ideas, I was sure this was not his first year doing this. I was interested to see how much response he got from the merchants.

Sam spent the remainder of the day in the office contacting stores to line them up for donations. Gene went back to his family. Billy came to the theater to pick me up to go to his place. While he was there, Sam secured the service of his van for Monday.

*

Billy and Sherry had a nice trailer house in a park at the edge of Boise. It was already decorated for Christmas on the inside, and presents lay under the tree. They let me take a shower in the spare bathroom, and I took my time under the hot water.

Then we ate lunch. Sherry had cooked a stew that was much better than any stew I had eaten on the trip, including the canned stew we had opened that first night in New Mexico, which now seemed so long ago.

We had good visit. They asked me about Texas and my family. I was guarded with my answers in case they were pumping me for information for Sam. I liked them, but I could not fully trust anyone. I didn't know what he had told them. I was afraid I would say something wrong, and he would punish me. Still, I enjoyed being with them and felt bad about my suspicions.

Sam came to get me and gave me orders to sweep and clean up the theater the following morning. Then he dropped me off at the theater and drove off.

Chapter Eighteen

Sam had preached his best sermons the first week. But since the offerings were constantly small, I wondered when the "give unto the Lord" messages would start.

I did not have to wait long. By Monday of the second week, he started preaching hard about money. Even my organ playing and Gene's guitar couldn't tickle the ears enough to lessen the blow. Crowds got smaller every night.

I normally had a couple of hours before Sam, Gene, and the others showed up in the morning. I didn't venture far from the theater, but sometimes I would go to the convenience store on the main street to get a cupcake. Or I would go to a small café I had found on the block across the main street to get some breakfast, normally consisting of a roll and hot chocolate or coffee. I was beginning to like coffee more, but still did not want it all the time. After breakfast, I would check the furnace and play the instruments.

The thing about being by yourself is that you have a lot of time to think about the situations you find yourself in. I had a lot of time to think and a lot to think about.

Besides my thoughts of going home, I still hoped to buy Gene's 'Cuda. He and Sam had managed to buy three cars to sell. Gene decided to keep one. It was a pretty light-blue 1967 Ford Galaxy. It was a nice car, kind of sporty. The Barracuda was a little small for his family, and he had not had a chance to replace the Fury he had to sell in Laramie. I saw this as a step closer to buying the 'Cuda for myself.

*

Before the Thursday night service, I came down the projector room stairs and Dorie was standing in the foyer. She was in a dark-blue dress, which made her blonde hair look very striking. She was a beautiful girl. She smiled when she saw me. As people walked in, I made my way over to her.

"Hi, Lee," she said. "Have you been okay?"

"Hi. Yeah, I've been fine. It's good to see you. Did you come for the service?"

"Maybe. But first, come outside with me."

I followed her out, glancing around to see if anyone was watching. Sam was not in sight. I didn't see Gene or anyone else on the team. A few of the gathering congregation looked at us as we made our way out to the sidewalk. *That's okay*, I thought. *They'll think she is my girlfriend.* The thought of it made me feel proud for a moment.

Once we got to the sidewalk, she turned and said, "I want you to meet someone." Then she took my hand and continued walking to a nice blue Ford LTD, which was parked at the curb. Sue was standing at the car with a nicely dressed boy about our age.

"This is John. He's a friend of ours."

John held out his hand. "Hi, Lee. I've heard about you."

I shook his hand and was about to invite them all in when John said, "Hey, why don't you come with us for a few minutes?" He turned and stepped off the curb. Sue followed him to the driver's side. They got in.

Dorie stepped toward me. "Can you? We're just going riding around."

I looked at the theater. "Well, service starts in a few minutes. I'd better not," I replied.

I knew I had about twenty minutes, and I was very tempted to go. If they were just going riding around Meridian, we would be back in plenty of time for the service. Standing there looking into Dorie's blue eyes wasn't helping. She clearly wanted me to go.

I watched her get into the car and started to follow her in.

Just then I heard a familiar voice behind me. "Where are you going, Lee?" Sam asked.

"They want me to go for a ride. We'll be back before the service."

"No, you don't have time to go anywhere. You'd better get in here and make sure everything is ready on stage. You should be playing as people come in."

I glared at him, knowing that he was just trying to get me inside, away from people my age, back inside where he could watch me and make sure I was there to help play my part of his game for the people. He knew everything was fine on stage, and I had never made a practice of playing this early before the services started. My anger burned.

I turned to look back at Dorie, and the disappointment I saw in her eyes was more than I could bear. I looked down at the sidewalk and said, "Well, I guess you know I've got to get in there. I'm sorry. I'll see you around." I looked back at her. "Come back to see me, okay?"

"Okay, Lee," she said softly. "I'll see you later." I closed the door for her. Then John started the car, and they sped off.

Back inside, I walked up the steps to the stage. I sat on the organ bench for a full five minutes before I started playing. Sam, at the back of the auditorium, was looking at me like he would like to strangle me. The feeling was mutual.

I lay on my cot that night wondering what I had missed. Were they just trying to get me away from there for a while for some good clean fun with kids my own age? Or were they not really good kids and trying to lure me away for more dangerous things? They did not have the appearance of bad kids, and I had no reason to think they were up to no good. John was apparently driving his parent's car—no teenager I knew would *buy* a big LTD. The day I had first met Dorie and Sue, they struck me as very nice girls who were friendly and curious about what was going on at the neighborhood theater they had probably seen all their lives. And with the looks Dorie gave me, I felt like she was genuinely interested in me. Maybe she sensed that I was in danger, and she wanted to help me get away. That was an interesting thought.

I could sure use some friends I could trust, I thought. *I'd like to talk to someone about this situation. I don't know that it would help, but it might give me another perspective that I can't see. All I know for sure is that I missed something tonight—some kind of activity with someone my own age.*

I knew for sure that God had been watching out for me on this trip, and I was thankful. After all, I had a mama back in Texas who I knew was praying for me every day. I knew God heard those prayers. If He had not allowed me to go with Dorie and her friends because they were trying to lure me into something bad, I was equally thankful. But I wrestled with the fact that maybe Dorie really felt something for me. *She sure looked disappointed when I had to stay,* I thought. *Maybe they will come back during the day when I would have time to go somewhere with them. That would be nice.*

I drifted off to sleep hoping I'd see her soon.

During the night the furnace went out again. I went through the same routine as before.

*

It snowed Friday in the late evening and got very cold. Not many people showed up for the service. Billy and Sherry were there. We visited after the service, and they made arrangements to pick me up the following day to spend some time at their house.

I noticed the accordion player was at the service and saw her talking to Gene and Donna afterwards.

Sunday night was to be the final service, and I was glad. That meant I was close to going home, if Sam held to his own bargain.

115

After everyone left, I took a chair outside and sat under the marquee and watched the snowfall. It was peaceful in Meridian, especially at that time of night. That night the streets were empty, allowing the blanket of snow to fall undisturbed.

Chapter Nineteen

I really liked the feeling of independence I had in Meridian. Except for working with the furnace, I enjoyed my surroundings at the Roxy. I was miles away from Sam, his screaming kids, and his confused wife. I was away from Gene and his family, and I knew they needed some time to themselves. The projector room was not a bad place, and the outside door to the balcony above the marquee was one of my favorite features of the place. I had grown accustomed to waking up early and standing on the balcony as the town was beginning to wake up. The businesses would open for the day, and sometimes a few people from the neighboring houses walked along the sidewalk in front of the theater. Sometimes they would see me and speak. I'm sure I was a sight, just rising, my long hair tousled and covered with smoke from the furnace.

Saturday morning I opened the door to the balcony and stepped into seven inches of beautiful snow. The snow crunched under my feet. The air was very cold and crisp, and it made me feel refreshed. It was simply beautiful. I wished I could take a picture and send it home. We didn't have scenes like this in Texas. I just stood there, leaning against the building and watching the people move slowly past on Main Street. I decided I might go to the five-and-dime on the corner and look at record albums. Although I had no money to buy any, I enjoyed looking at the pictures on the cover and seeing what the groups that I had heard on the radio looked like. I would have to wait until everyone left that afternoon to go. I was sure we would be busy picking up donations that day.

Billy picked me up mid-morning. As we went from place to place to pick up toys and food, he talked of how he liked his van, how good it handled in the snow, and how much room it had to haul people around.

I liked being with him. He had a pleasant personality. I wondered how it might be to work with him in the youth ministry. I sort of hoped he would ask me what I thought about it, but he didn't.

We picked up the things offered by the merchants and individuals on our list and headed back to the theater to unload. I had a good feeling when I saw how much we were collecting to help people during the holidays. Toys were everywhere. An electric racetrack lay in a box on the floor in front of the counter. Teddy bears, dolls, fire trucks, dump trucks—it seemed like every kind of toy ever made waited to be picked up by some happy kid on Christmas morning. I thought of my nephews back home. *I bet they would like some of these.* Merchants had donated a lot of canned food, too. I spotted a can of orange cake frosting. I had never seen canned frosting. Mama always made hers from scratch. *Boy,* I thought, *what I would give for a couple of slices of her German chocolate cake about now!*

I knew my family back home in Texas would all be getting together during the upcoming holidays. We always did. It would be my first time to not be with them. When I left Texas in August I felt like I was taking a positive step, even if it was for all the wrong reasons. But it was nearing Christmas, and I was very homesick for my family and friends back home. Thanksgiving had not been observed on this trip. Christmas would be hard if I was not at home.

Maybe I could handle being back at home now, even if it wasn't a perfect world. This sure wasn't one, either.

I was lonely for some friends my age. Other than Dorie, Sue, and John, I had met no one even close. All of the people I was with at least had their families with them. I had no one.

*

Gene came Sunday morning as I was sweeping the floor of the auditorium. He laughed when he saw me pushing the broom.

"Well, guess what we're going to do now," Gene said, his countenance changing a bit.

"What?" I asked. *I'm going home,* I thought to myself.

"Sam is getting us some uniforms."

"What kind of uniforms? What for?"

"Starting Monday night, we're going to stand in front of the mall in Boise to collect money for under-privileged children. He's getting us uniforms like the

119

Salvation Army, except we're going by 'The Lord's Army.' He said we would get a percentage of the money we bring in. That's how he's going to pay us, since the offerings were low."

That beat all I'd ever heard! I'd done some strange things, but begging strangers for money wasn't one of them. I tried to imagine standing at a mall entrance with a tin cup.

I stared at Gene as thoughts whirled through my head. *How we're getting paid? Oh, he means him and the others. Sam's taking some of the money and buying my bus ticket and giving me some to eat on.*

Then it occurred to me that Gene had said "we" as if he was including me in on the deal. "He's not getting me a uniform, is he?" I tried to read his face as I spoke the rest of my thoughts. "I *am* going home, aren't I?"

Gene looked at the floor. "I don't know."

My heart sank. That was a pretty good indication that he knew more than I did about it. Still, I tried to think optimistically. *Gene can't know everything about everything*, I thought. I decided I'd wait to see what Sam said.

"Oh, yeah." Gene interrupted my thoughts. "Ellen and Pam are going back home to Laramie. Sam told her she would have to go to the mall with us, and she balked!" He laughed.

"Good," I said. "That lady really got on my nerves."

"Hey, you know that little café you told me about on the next block over?"

"Yeah," I answered.

"Well, I went there to get coffee just now. Did you know the back of it opens up to a bar after hours?"

"No, I didn't." I really had not noticed anything about it when I was there. It was just a café to me.

"Well, it does. And there is a poster of the band playing there next weekend. The bandleader is a friend of mine. I knew him years ago back home."

"Huh! Are you going to go see him?"

"Maybe. I don't know."

"Well, you should. I bet he'd be surprised."

"Yeah, I bet."

I could tell he would like to see him. But I also knew he shouldn't be seen at a bar. Church people wouldn't understand. We were trying to help people in the area. We had to keep a good reputation.

*

Sam came in later with three uniforms—one for Gene, one for Donna, and one for me.

I asked, trying to stay calm, "Why did you get me a uniform? Aren't I going home? You said I could."

"Lee," he said, "don't you know we didn't get much offering from these people? I don't have the money to send you home. If I did, I'd let you go for good! If you bring in a lot at the mall, maybe you can get enough to buy your own ticket. We'll see."

At that, he went into his office and shut the door. I started to follow him in but decided to go to the projector room instead.

I should have known this would happen, I thought as I stomped up the stairs. *I am stuck here. He will never let me go, no matter what he promised.*

Then I remembered what Gene had said about a percentage of the money. *If he really gives us a percentage, maybe I could get enough money to buy my own ticket. Then I would go home all right—for good!*

I started a letter to Mama. I had to keep her thinking I was trying to get out of there. I told her about soliciting at the mall and how I'd get the money from that to come home. Even as I wrote, I had my doubts.

*

It snowed again on Monday. It was bitterly cold. We were dropped off late that afternoon at separate mall entrances and told to stand inside the first set of doors.

I tromped up to the entrance I was assigned to. Standing just inside the big glass doors with a tambourine and a bucket, I felt very uncomfortable and ashamed. Not only were my feet getting numb from the cold, but also the cold stares from the Christmas shoppers entering the mall made a chill run up my spine. How dare I ask for money at a time when they were scurrying about buying gifts for their families! And I couldn't blame them.

I took a break after an hour or so. I was about to sit down on a chair in the mall when I heard Gene call to me. He and Donna were walking my way.

"Hey, we found a place to get hot chocolate. Do you want some?"

"Yes, I do. I'm about to freeze! I don't like this at all."

"Neither do we," Donna said. "But this may get us a little money so we can eat. That will be worth it."

"Yeah, I guess so." I knew she was right.

We were picked up just before the mall closed—and just before I froze solid, it felt like. My toes were in worst shape than my legs, and my legs were tingling every time I moved. My gloves could not keep my fingers warm, and my cheeks felt like chunks of ice.

I had collected very little, in spite of my efforts to smile and be friendly all evening.

Sam took us the next day to buy some insulated boots. I saw a thick winter hat with earflaps and decided to buy it. The boots helped keep feeling in my toes that second night. The hat protected my ears and cheeks.

Even though I had started a letter to Mama, I called home Wednesday from the pay phone by the café. Mama could hear my voice quivering, and she thought I was scared. I told her I was just cold, and then I told her it was fifteen degrees below zero. She could not imagine anyone being out in that kind of temperature. I told her the weather was very cold and snow covered the ground constantly, and that I had never been in a place as cold or snowy. I assured her I had on a heavy coat, two pair of pants, socks, and shirts when I went out. She told me to get inside somewhere.

Before I hung up, I told her about the mall soliciting.

"This looks like the only way I am going to get the money to come home, Mama. I will come home as soon as I can. I just can't let Sam know I plan to."

"But will he find out and hurt you?"

"No, I won't let that happen. I've got to go. Just don't worry about me, okay?"

"Well, okay, Son. Be careful."

"I will. Bye."

*

The routine became a grind. During the day Sam would call around to stores for contributions of food, toys, and anything else for the Lord's Army. Billy, Gene, and I would then go to the stores to collect. The foyer of the theater got so full that it was hard to walk through. Sam kept the money stashed somewhere.

I was growing increasingly tired of the cold and the looks and comments of the people as they read the sign on the bucket: "Please Give to Underprivileged Children." Some people looked at me and smiled as they walked by. Some folks ignored me. Several would give a little bit of change or let their children put some in the bucket. One guy sneered as he passed, then turned around and threw a quarter at my bucket and said sharply, "Here, go buy yourself a beer!" Then he was gone. It bothered me. I was not an angel, but I didn't waste my money—or anyone else's—on alcohol. I'd seen at home what that does to a person, a family, and I wanted no part of it—ever.

Chapter Twenty

Saturday, Gene told me he had gone to see Danny at the café after he'd let me off at the theater Friday night. They had a good time visiting, he said.

I decided to go see the band for myself that night. I went there for a cup of coffee and a piece of pie after we got back from the mall. As I walked in, I heard the music coming from the wide-open doors at the back of the room. I sat at the café counter and ordered. I overheard a couple of women at the end of the counter talking and gathered that one of them was Danny's wife. So I interrupted their conversation.

"Are you Danny's wife?"

They looked at me, and the one sitting closest to me said, "Well, yeah. And who are you?"

"I'm a friend of Gene Trail's. He told me he was a friend of Danny's."

"Yeah, we know Gene. He was in here last night, and we were surprised to see him." She looked me over. "So, you are traveling in the same outfit he's in?"

"Yeah, we're up here with a revival team."

"Well, I'll tell Danny you're here. He'll want to meet you, I'm sure, since you are a friend of Gene's. Hang on."

She got up and went through the open doors. At the end of the song she went to the steel guitar player. She leaned over him and said something in his ear. I saw his eyes look my direction. He motioned for me to go in and sit at a table. I had not intended for it to go this way. I did not want to go into the bar. I waved and smiled at him, and he kept on motioning for me. Then he said something to his wife, and she came to me.

"Danny wants you to go sit down and listen to them." She saw my hesitation and laughed. "Well, come on!"

"Okay," I reluctantly went on in. *Meridian has sure been a place for a lot of "firsts" for me!* I thought. *Add this one to the list.*

I walked through the open doors into a small room that had about the same number of tables as the adjacent café. They lined the walls in order to give room for dancing in the center of the room. Five or six couples of all ages were seated. About that many more were dancing, or trying to. I'd never seen anyone dance in person, but the ones I had seen on TV could at least stand up straight when they wanted. Most of these people, I presumed, were plastered or well on their way. I felt seriously out of place. And dangerously out of place, considering my age.

Danny whispered something to a cute waitress, and she came to my table and asked what I wanted to drink. I said water would be fine. She laughed and said, "You don't understand. Danny's buying, and he said to give you anything you want."

I looked up at this girl who was barely older than me, it seemed, and I wondered how she came to be a waitress here. "Oh, thanks, but I don't want anything, really. Water's fine."

She shook her head and smiled at me. "Okay, I'll get you some water, but if you change your mind, he's buying!"

"Okay, thanks."

I sat there and watched the band play. It was rather comical that several times during every song Danny would have to pull his steel guitar back to him because as he played it would move away from him on the slick wooden floor. I laughed to myself every time. He made a joke about it after one song, saying, "You ladies are having so much fun out there, you are making my steel guitar want to dance!"

But as I watched the patrons trip over each other dancing, I decided that I could never feel comfortable in a place like a bar. It brought back too many bad memories of life at home, and I just did not like the atmosphere.

Danny came and sat at my table during a break, and we chatted about Gene and music.

"It's always nice to see Gene. I was a little surprised to see him up here, though! We go back a long ways. And it's nice to meet you, Lee."

"Good to meet you, too." I said, excited to meet someone who actually made a living with his music.

"So, he said you folks were up here with a preacher. Something about a theater..." He looked at me as if he wanted me to tell him some more.

I told him a short version, leaving out the part about my personal problems with the preacher.

"Sounds like it's a busy outfit," he said.

"Yeah, it has been a hoot!" I returned, wishing I could tell him more but knowing it would not matter in the end.

As he got up at the end of the break, he invited me to come back the next weekend and sit in with them on bass guitar. I told him I might do that. I really had no intentions of going back.

I glanced through the window and saw a policeman drive buy. My heart leaped in my chest. I sure didn't need to be found in a bar at my age. He drove on by, and I settled back down as the band played another song. Knowing I had seen and heard enough, I stood and waved to Danny, then I walked through the café and out the front door.

I told Gene the next day about going to meet Danny, and he told me I shouldn't go back.

"I know, but he asked me to sit in with the band and play bass. That would be fun."

"Yeah, but I don't want to have to pick you up at the jail because you—a minor—got caught in a bar. Then if Sam found out—! Just forget it." Gene had never been that stern to me—not even the few times I had gotten into small arguments with his kids about various things. I knew he was right, and the fact that he was so stern made me decide for sure not to go back.

*

On Monday, the 11th of December, the temperature reached nineteen below zero. I thought I'd freeze to death for sure standing there at the mall.

Tuesday morning, I put on three layers of clothing and stood on the balcony looking at the fire station. I had an idea. There was one sure way to get home. I could break the law and make sure I got caught. I thought of several things I could try: shoplifting at the variety store on the corner; ripping off a piece of candy at the grocery store; pumping some gas at the station and driving off—boy, that would do it! They would hang me high for driving without a license, stealing gas, and whatever else they could think of. Maybe I would have to spend some time behind bars. No, that didn't sound too good! I had never been in trouble with the law, and I couldn't start now. Besides, I'd have to tell them who I was with so far from home, and when Sam found out, he'd kill me for sure.

I shook my head to clear out those thoughts, turned, and walked back inside. No use—I was trapped. My only hope was the promise about my cut of the money collected at the mall.

I did decide to try one tactic akin to a lawbreaker, though. Later that day, I left the Roxy to walk around. I saw a cop driving towards me. I waited until he got close, then I quickly raised my right hand to my brow to cover my face, as if I didn't want him to see me. Maybe he would think I was acting suspicious and stop to check me out. I kept walking as he passed. He kept driving. I heard no sliding of tires, no hollering "stop" from anywhere behind me. Nothing. I had failed.

Chapter Twenty-One

On the 14th of December, Gene pulled up in front of the theater. He stood outside and lit up a cigarette. He took a few drags and threw it down. I met him as he came in the door. He looked worried.

"What's wrong?" I asked. I wasn't used to seeing this worried look on him.

"Sam packed up his family, took the money, and went to Oregon. Left us flat. He gave me one hundred dollars and told me he would be back in two weeks."

"What? Well, that sorry bum. What are we supposed to do? Keep going to the mall and collecting money?"

"No. We will not go back out there. But we have to do something. I can't take care of everybody on a hundred lousy bucks. He's gone too far this time. I don't know what we are going to do, but we can't sit around here."

We stood there and looked at each other for a moment. I didn't know what else to say. I saw the opportunity to catch a bus and get home. I had one hundred and seventy-five dollars saved up from the mall soliciting, and that should get me to Texas, with food in my stomach and warm clothes on my back. But I really wanted to know what he was thinking. *Can I leave him here like Sam did? Would that be right, after all he's done for me?* I pondered that for a long moment as we stood there in the cold.

Gene looked around at the goods in the foyer. "I'll think of something. I'll get back to you later. Just stay in the theater and keep warm." With that, he got in his Galaxy and drove back to his family at the edge of town.

I sat in one of the back seats of the theater for a long time, thinking about what I should do. I thought about the food, clothing, and toys that sat on the counter and floor of the foyer and about the money we had taken from the people in the Boise/Meridian area.

Just how much money did he take with him to Oregon? I wondered. *Leaving us one hundred dollars to do what we could. So, was this his plan all along? Had he dreamed this whole trip up so that he and his precious family could spend Christmas in Oregon? Why else would we end up in a place where the snow is fifteen inches deep and the temperature is lower than anyone from the south should ever be in?*

I dozed off there, sunk down in the chair. When I woke up, I didn't know how long I had been there, but it was dark outside. I climbed the stairs and fell into a fitful sleep.

*

Gene came mid-morning and found me stoking coal in the furnace.

"Forget that," he said. "You're going to stay Billy's for a couple of days. I think I'm going to be able to get you home for Christmas."

I stared at him. "How?" I asked.

"Well, I don't have everything worked out yet, but do you still want the 'Cuda?"

"Well, yeah, I do. But for how much?"

"If you can give me a hundred cash, we'll call it even. Do you have that much?"

My heart leaped! "Yeah, I do. That's cool." I dug out the money before he changed his mind. That would leave me seventy-five dollars. Home or not, the 'Cuda was about to be mine.

"Deal," I said as I handed him the money.

"All right. Get your stuff and come with me. And don't talk about this with anyone." He took the money and headed out the door.

*

At Billy and Sherry's, I managed to get some guarded relaxation. I didn't know how much they knew about anything. Did they still trust Sam? Had they figured him out? I only knew I had to keep quiet about what I knew.

"So, what are your plans, Lee, now that Sam is in Oregon?" Billy asked me at supper.

"I don't know, I guess. I'd like to go home—just for Christmas. But I don't see how I can." I played ignorant, hoping they would think I would be ready to come back after Christmas, just in case they talked to Sam.

They must have been talking to him some, because Sherry said softly, "Well, Lee, I know Sam is hoping you will join them in Oregon." She smiled, and I studied her face. It had a kind, gentle, Christian look to it. I could not detect any evil in her at all. I was pretty sure he still had them snookered.

"We'll see," I answered. I said nothing else about it.

The phone rang early the following morning.

"Sam wants to speak to you, Lee," Sherry said, holding the receiver in my direction.

"Hello," I said into the phone.

"Hey, Bud, how are you?" he asked in a cheery voice.

"I'm all right," I answered.

"Man, you ought to be here with me. This place is a beauty."

"Really?" I tried to sound interested.

"Yeah, man, it really is. I'm hoping you will join us out here. I'll come and get you if you want to."

"Well, I don't know." I left the decision hanging.

"What do you want to do? I know you'd like to be home at Christmas. What are your plans?"

Is he baiting me? I thought to myself. *How would he think I'd get home? With part of the money he left behind? Fat chance!*

"My folks don't have money to send me to get home on. I am trying to find a way, but I haven't yet." I wanted to play his cat-and-mouse game a while longer, trying to get to the depth of what he was trying to say. I could not believe he would let me go that easy. It just didn't seem likely, unless I was right about his ultimate plan—to get to Oregon for the holidays. A life-long fantasy, maybe? Who knew?

"Well, whatever you decide, I'll go along with it," he said. I could read nothing from his voice. "I'll talk to you

134

later. If you decide to come out here, Billy knows where I am. Just call me. See ya, Bud." And he was gone.

I hung up the phone as confused as before.

Gene came over early in the afternoon. "Hi. How are you guys?" he asked cheerfully.

"Fine." All three of us spoke in unison.

"Lee, I need you to come with me to straighten up things at the theater."

"Okay." I pulled on my snow boots and grabbed my coat.

"I'll be back after a while," I said as I headed out the door.

"I don't know; we may get done late," Gene interrupted. "Why don't you plan to stay with us tonight, Lee?"

"Okay," I answered, catching his tone. I threw a glance at Billy and Sherry and shrugged. Then I shut the door.

As we headed for the theater, I told Gene about the conversation with Sam.

"Well, I don't know what he's up to, but I have my own plan. You can come with me or go to him."

He laid out the plans to me. "We are leaving in the morning. Janet wants to come with us." He looked at me straight in the eyes, and he saw my reaction before I spoke.

"Janet?" I shrieked. I did not like the accordion player, and I did not want her go with us. "Why does she want to go with us?"

Gene shrugged. "I don't know. She said she wants to go to Texas. Said she'll go with us as far as we'll let her go. She said she'll let us sell her car to get the money to head out of town."

Knowing we needed all the money we could get, I said, "Well, I'm going with you. And I'll be nice to her since she's selling her car to help. Let's go!"

I remembered the conversation with Sam. It dawned on me that Sam did not matter any more. I was finally going home.

Chapter Twenty-Two

We decided to load up the instruments and take them to the trailer.

"I really don't want to leave them in the theater," Gene said. "I think we ought to put everything together."

I told him, "We ought to keep the guitars, Gene, because Sam really owes us at least what they are worth. I know you really like the Baldwin, and I would love to have that Vox."

I thought he was going to agree, but he didn't. "It would just be something for him to accuse us of stealing," he said.

I knew he was right, but I still thought we wouldn't be wrong in taking them.

"We'll take the stuff to the trailer early in the morning before everybody wakes up. Then we'll meet everyone else at the my trailer and pull out." He had planned everything out.

Early Tuesday morning, the 17th of December, after we took the instruments to the trailer, I loaded my clothes, shoes, and my cherished record into the back of the Barracuda. As I looked around the foyer of the Roxy, I thought of my nephews who would be at my house for Christmas, and I grabbed a few toys to give them as gifts. I also picked up an extra jacket for myself. Then I grabbed another can of cake frosting to eat on the way.

I regretted not being able to say good-bye to Billy and Sherry. They had been nice to me, and I felt they had been innocent of any wrongdoing. They deserved a final word of thanks. But we could not take the chance that they might tell Sam.

I also regretted not being able to tell Dorie I was leaving. I would now have to eternally wonder about her thoughts of me.

We were headed out of town by 7:30 a.m. The weather was bitterly cold. Snow and ice covered everything. I wanted to get out of all of it and get to Texas. Gene drove his Galaxy and pulled my 'Cuda. Donna and two of the kids rode with him. Janet drove her car, and I rode with her and the two oldest kids.

We drove south into Utah. We stayed off the main highway in case Sam found out we were gone and chased us. Because of that, we had to drive through more severe road conditions than we would have otherwise. We drove behind Gene, and when we crossed the icy bridges, I watched wide-eyed as my car swayed on the ice. He was a careful driver, but with the bridges frozen solid, the tires had nothing to grab onto. I was glad Janet was used to driving in those conditions. I began to be thankful that she was traveling with us.

I prayed a lot through those mountains. I prayed for our safety, for the cars to stay straight on the roads, and that I would finally make it home. I made a few promises, too: I promised to be good, to try to get along with Daddy, and to treat Mama with more respect and help her more than ever.

I had not phoned my folks to tell them we were on the way. I figured I would wait until we were almost home, in case the weather held us up on the way. I had no idea how long it would take to get home in the ice and snow. I knew it had taken us five days to get to Laramie from Texas in good weather, but part of that was because of all the trouble we had with the bus. Just the same, I figured it would be best to have them think I was still buckled down in Meridian. My mind raced ahead of us, wondering just what I would find at home. Would it be easier now?

On the evening of the second day, traffic was almost shut down because of the ice. We pulled into the parking lot of a truck stop. It was a solid sheet of ice. Trucks were sitting everywhere, engines running, truckers walking back and forth, pausing to converse and shake their heads in frustration at the weather.

Gene walked and slid to the car I was in. "I think we'll stay here tonight. I'm going to talk to some of these guys and see how it is further on. Why don't you come with me, Lee."

Glad to get out of the car for a while, I followed him to a group of guys standing in the sub-zero evening drinking huge cups of steaming coffee. Most, I noticed, were smoking cigarettes.

I stuck close to Gene and listened.

"How far south is this weather like this?" Gene asked the group.

"To about Ogden it's mostly ice," one trucker said.

The others agreed.

Before long, I was eager to get out of the cold wind. I left them talking and rushed back to the car, sliding through the icy ruts created by the wheels of the big trucks.

We followed the same pattern for three days. We drove through mountain passes that were solid ice. It took forever to get anywhere. At mealtime we would stop at roadside parks and picnic areas, pile into one car, and fix sandwiches. We slept sitting up in the Galaxy, snuggling against one another to stay warm. Gene would leave the car running with the heater on. He would wake up once in a while and turn it off to conserve fuel, then wake up again and start it again when he got cold. It was very uncomfortable, but renting motel rooms was out of the question. We were just glad to be headed south.

By the time we got to Ogden, the roads were clear. We sold Janet's car to a garage owner there. It amazed me to see Gene just walk up a greasy driveway into a small garage, walk out with a man in greasy overalls, show him the '58 Chevy, and sell it to him right on the spot. I was impressed once again at Gene's wisdom in dealing with people.

From there on, Gene allowed me to drive my 'Cuda at times to relieve Donna. Sometimes, however, we would pull it to save gas, and we'd all cramp up in the Galaxy.

By late afternoon on Friday we had pulled into central New Mexico. We stopped at truck stop to eat a hot supper. Gene said I would be home in about twenty-four hours, so I decided to call home.

My mom answered the phone. "Hello."

"Hi, Mama."

"Hi, Son. We were wondering when you would call again," she said in her familiar worried voice.

"I'm on the way home, Mama." I paused, waiting for her reaction.

She gasped. "You are?" I could almost see her smiling as she asked me.

"Yeah. We're in New Mexico, and I should be there sometime tomorrow night, if we don't hit any bad weather. Are any of the girls there yet?"

"No. They are coming tomorrow morning. I'm so glad you're coming home." She started crying. Daddy grabbed the phone.

"You're coming home, Son?" he asked, having over-heard Mama's words. "When will you be here?" he continued.

As homesick as I was, I still wasn't comfortable talking to Daddy. I gritted my teeth and kept talking, mainly so he could tell my sisters when they got there the next day.

"Daddy, I was telling Mama that I should be home late tomorrow afternoon if the weather holds. We're in New Mexico. Gene and his family are bringing me home. We ran away from Sam on the seventeenth. Has he called? I'm sure that by now he knows we're gone. Don't tell him where we are if he calls."

"No, he hasn't called. You just get home. And be careful."

"All right. I'll see you tomorrow night. I've gotta go; they're waiting on me. Bye."

Gene was behind me when I hung up the phone. "Everything okay?" he asked.

"Yeah, it's cool." I said. "Let's get to Texas!"

141

Chapter Twenty-Three

I'll never forget the feeling of relief I felt as we topped a hill several miles from Abilene in the late evening on the 23rd of December and I saw the lights of the town. I felt so much joy inside to be getting back home. Even if home would be the same as it was before I left, at least I would not be hundreds of miles away from everyone who meant anything to me.

At 10:00 p.m., we pulled up in front of my house. I got out of the car. I was dirty from six days on the road. I was equally tired and hungry. My hair had grown out longer than my family had ever seen it. I dreaded their comments about it. But I did not regret finally growing it the way I wanted to.

I stood at the road, looking at the old rock house. It had never looked as inviting to me as it did at that moment. Three cars besides my parents Falcon wagon sat in front of the house, and I knew everybody was there.

"I'll unhook your car," Gene said. "You go see your family."

I walked cautiously up to the house. Gene leaned up against his car and watched. No one else got out.

I couldn't help but wonder whether or not they would all be glad to see me. I knocked on the front door like a stranger. I could hear the voices of my sisters, brothers-in-law, and nephews inside.

It got quiet. My brother-in-law Don opened the door. He stood there looking at me for a long moment. As I looked at him I saw my sisters and nephews gather into the room behind him. They just stood and looked me over. I couldn't blame them. I had lost weight. My face was bony. And with my dirty long hair, I had to be a sickening sight.

Finally I said, "Hi."

They all looked at each other questioningly. Then they all came and hugged me and told me it was good to have me home. I held onto each of them like I would never let them go. Mama came into the room. They all stepped aside and motioned for me to go to her. I knew the past few months had been as hard on her as they had for me, and harder in some ways. I was her baby, a prodigal son of sorts. It did not matter how dirty I was. I knew Mama would just be glad to see me home.

She looked weak and pale. She held onto me for a long moment and cried.

Back outside, I called to Gene to come to meet the family. He didn't know how he would be accepted.

My brothers-in-law followed me out. Wayne spoke up. "Thanks for getting him home. I guess it's been a long drive." He reached out to shake Gene's hand. Gene responded silently by taking his hand with a firm grip and nodding a greeting.

My brothers-in-law went back in, and I said good-bye to everyone. I hugged all the kids, Donna, and Gene. I thanked them for everything. But how could I say enough words to express my thankfulness for the kindness shown to me by this family? For the past five months Gene had helped me through a lot of bad situations. He had calmed me down when I was angry. He had protected me from a lot of danger—and probably some I didn't even know about. He and Donna had fed me and washed my laundry like I was one of their own. And, finally, they had gotten me home.

I stood at the road waving as they left.

But they left Janet.

"She says this is where she feels she needs to be," Gene had explained. "Maybe your family could put her up for the night, and she'll find someplace tomorrow. I don't know."

I didn't know either. My family was glad to see me home, but I didn't know if they would accept a strange woman in the house.

"Come on in, Janet. I'll see what we can do." I didn't know *what* to do. She followed me in.

"Mom, everyone, this is Janet. She came with us from Meridian. She wanted to try Texas out for a while, and she sold her car on the way to help us get home." I realized that I really knew nothing more about her than what I had said, other than the fact that she was an accordion player—and knowing *that* would not help her case any. But I thought if I could tell them something to thank her for, maybe it would be easier for them to answer my next question.

"Can she stay the night? She can find some other place tomorrow."

It really didn't work. They were polite to her, but after some discussion in the kitchen, they decided against it. It was too much for them to deal with right here at Christmas.

I didn't care. I was home, and the sooner I could put that entire trip behind me, the better off I would be.

Wayne and I took her to a shelter in town. We said our good-byes and went our separate ways.

After visiting with the family for a long while, I said goodnight and went to my room. As I lay down on the bed, I looked around at the pictures, models, and furnishings, all of which were just as I had left them. I felt like I had been away from home in a war. I was so glad to be back. There had been some good times on my trip, and the memories of those would get clearer in my mind later. For now, I was in my own bed and close to my own family.

I thought of the look on Mama's face as she reached for me. All the prayers she had prayed for me in the last several months had been answered. All the tears she had cried were seen in heaven—and, knowing Mama as I did, I knew that there had been so many that some were still there, bottled up for future times of need.

I was back where I needed to be. I knew I would not leave with strangers again. I knew Mama had prayed me home.

Afterword

Two days after I returned home, Daddy was admitted to a local hospital. He passed away on the 3rd of January. In the months that followed, Mama arranged to move closer to Fort Worth. There I met the girl who would become my wife.

A preacher's daughter, she had grown up strong in character and morals, and God knew she would be able to help me with the issues and attitudes I had to work through because of my rebellion. We are now in our thirty-first year of a wonderful marriage. We were blessed with two very talented sons who are raising their own families and serving the Lord in music ministry.

I now have no hang-ups because of what happened to me during my time at home or during the five months I was kidnapped. I have lived a great life, have a great family, and I love God with all my heart. I hold no ill feelings for the preacher who took me. I only hope he saw his mistakes at some point and made things right in his heart. And I do not want anyone to think that I think badly of preachers. I don't! Some of my best friends today are preachers, and there are several in my family.

I know for a fact that trials and tests of life have helped mold me into who I am today. I know I learned some good lessons on my trip with the evangelist. One thing I learned for sure was something I had heard all my life: "Never go with strangers." We see people every day who have lost their way. We have to be alert for our safety and sensitive to God's leading.

I was grown before I even tried to understand how my dad lived as he did. I forgave him a long time ago. Unfortunately, it was years after his death. I was told he made things right with God before he passed. I hope to see him in heaven.

*

Thank you for taking the time to read this book. It is my account of a personal experience—seen through my eyes. No one else lived it like I did. No one else has the memories I have relived over and over again through the years. Many of them became clearer as I wrote this book. A great number of the details were gleaned from letters and notes I have kept in my possession. A great many more have been bouncing back and forth in my head for thirty-one years. I hope it blessed you.

In closing, I have one request to make of you: Keep praying for your family and those you see in need!

God bless you,
Lee Sturgeon